A PRACTICAL GUIDE TO HAPPINESS IN ADULTS ON THE AUTISM SPECTRUM

by the same author

A Practical Guide to Happiness in Children and Teens on the Autism Spectrum
A Positive Psychology Approach
Victoria Honeybourne
ISBN 978 1 78592 347 0
eISBN 978 1 78450 681 0

The Neurodiverse Classroom
A Teacher's Guide to Individual Learning Needs and How to Meet Them
Victoria Honeybourne
ISBN 978 1 78592 362 3
eISBN 978 1 78450 703 9

of related interest

Autism and Enablement
Occupational Therapy Approaches to Promote Independence for Adults with Autism
Matt Bushell, Sandra Gasson and Ute Vann
ISBN 978 1 78592 087 5
eISBN 978 1 78450 348 2

Autism and Solution-focused Practice
Els Mattelin and Hannelore Volckaert
ISBN 978 1 78592 328 9
ISBN 978 1 78450 644 5

The Guide to Good Mental Health on the Autism Spectrum
Jeanette Purkis, Emma Goodall and Jane Nugent
Forewords by Wenn Lawson and Kirsty Dempster-Rivett
ISBN 978 1 84905 670 0
ISBN 978 1 78450 195 2

A PRACTICAL GUIDE TO HAPPINESS IN ADULTS ON THE AUTISM SPECTRUM

A POSITIVE PSYCHOLOGY APPROACH

Victoria Honeybourne

Jessica Kingsley *Publishers*
London and Philadelphia

First published in 2019
by Jessica Kingsley Publishers
73 Collier Street
London N1 9BE, UK
and
400 Market Street, Suite 400
Philadelphia, PA 19106, USA

www.jkp.com

Library of Congress Cataloging in Publication Data
Names: Honeybourne, Victoria (Language and communication teacher), author.
Title: A practical guide to happiness in adults on the autism spectrum : a
    positive psychology approach / Victoria Honeybourne.
Description: London ; Philadelphia : Jessica Kingsley Publishers, 2019. |
    Includes bibliographical references.
Identifiers: LCCN 2018024745 | ISBN 9781785925771
Subjects: LCSH: Autistic people--Psychology. | Autistic people--Mental
    health. | Happiness. | Positive psychology.
Classification: LCC RC553.A88 H66 2019 | DDC 616.85/882--
dc23 LC record available at https://lccn.loc.gov/2018024745

British Library Cataloguing in Publication Data
A CIP catalogue record for this book is available from the British Library

ISBN 978 1 78592 577 1
eISBN 978 1 78450 988 0

Printed and bound in Great Britain

The Appendices include printable resources to be used in
the activities, and they are available to download and print
from www.jkp.com/voucher using the code DYYVERE

CONTENTS

INTRODUCTION

What does it mean to be happy? We use the word 'happy' frequently – 'I just want my children to be happy', 'I'll be happy when this week is over', 'Are you happy in your new job?' – but what exactly do we mean by happiness? Is happiness a short-term state ('I'm happy when I'm playing tennis') or a longer-term condition ('I'm a happy person')? The very thing that makes one person extremely happy (going to a football match, reading a book, being alone...) might indeed induce a state of extreme unhappiness in another. But happiness, however defined, is something generally considered a positive state worth cultivating.

Every one of us experiences the world differently. We each interpret the world through our own unique eyes. This uniqueness makes life so wonderfully diverse – but can also be what causes so many misunderstandings and difficulties at times. Individual uniqueness means that what will make each of us happy will differ too. All too often research indicates that individuals on the autism spectrum are more likely to be unhappy, depressed, anxious or worried than neurotypical others. Perhaps too often we assume that the problem lies within those individuals, rather than viewing happiness as the multi-faceted construct it is, influenced heavily by social, environmental and psychological factors.

This book is a guide to promoting happiness and wellbeing in individuals on the autism spectrum (including those with Asperger syndrome) using a positive psychology approach. Positive psychology is the scientific, evidence-based study of the positive elements of human existence such as strengths, positive emotions and positive coping mechanisms. This book also considers wider related issues, such as the fundamentals of wellbeing and the importance of not imposing a neurotypical view of happiness on autistic individuals.

AIMS OF THIS BOOK

This book provides a starting point for applying some of the findings of positive psychology when working with adults on the autism spectrum (for more detailed information about specific aspects of positive psychology, please see the 'Further Reading and Resources' section). The following chapters aim to:

- Demonstrate how findings from the positive psychology movement can be used or adapted with individuals on the autism spectrum in order to improve their wellbeing and happiness

- Provide practical strategies and approaches for individuals on the autism spectrum to put into place in their own life

- Provide practical strategies and approaches for professionals to use when working with individuals on the autism spectrum in a range of settings

- Demonstrate the importance of not imposing a neurotypical view of happiness or current societal trends and values on individuals on the autism spectrum

Individuals on the autism spectrum can face a range of challenges in everyday life. Traditionally, 'success' has been measured for individuals on the autism spectrum in terms of tangible, physical outcomes – being in employment, for example, achieving a qualification, or living independently. Achieve those things, and the individual is deemed to be successful. Although these successes can be important, it does not necessarily follow that they automatically bring happiness and wellbeing too. An individual on the autism spectrum might be highly qualified, employed and live independently, but could simultaneously be extremely unhappy, unfulfilled, anxious and lonely. Research is beginning to show that success does not bring long-term happiness, but that being happy can increase the likelihood of success. This book is based on that philosophy: that individuals on the autism spectrum who have a good sense of wellbeing and happiness are in a far better position to be able to overcome any difficulties they might face, work towards their goals and make informed decisions based on their own strengths and values. This book explores the concept of happiness from various angles: How far does our internal self-talk affect our happiness? How do the people around us affect our happiness? What impact do the media have?

When it comes to lasting wellbeing and happiness, there are rarely 'quick fixes' to change an individual's outlook overnight. The activities and strategies suggested in this book are not intended to be one-off tasks, but rather to be starting points to initiate discussion and new ways of thinking. These are ongoing strategies that can be developed and extended over time to meet individual needs and circumstances. This is not a book that aims to make autistic people any less autistic – it is a book aimed at helping those on the autism spectrum to feel happier being who they are and to develop the resilience and skills needed to live an authentic life.

It is always difficult to design any book, resource or activity for individuals on the autism spectrum, for just that reason – autism is a spectrum, and one that is constantly evolving, expanding and extending. Individuals on the autism spectrum are found across the ability range, are from a range of backgrounds and have a range of attitudes, experiences and goals. Each individual will be at a different starting point in their journey in understanding who they are and how they relate to the people and society around them. Therefore, not every activity in this book will be appropriate for every individual on the autism spectrum. Individuals, or professionals working with individuals, should choose those activities that are most relevant.

REMEMBER! The activities in this book are designed to help individuals increase feelings of happiness and wellbeing. They are not a substitute for professional mental health input and are not designed to support individuals experiencing significant mental health difficulties. Individuals with acute and significant mental health needs should ask for a referral to local health services as soon as possible to receive specialised input.

NOTE! If you are working with young people, *A Practical Guide to Happiness in Children and Teens on the Autism Spectrum* (Jessica Kingsley Publishers 2017) by the same author focuses on specific issues and activities for this age group.

WHO THIS BOOK IS FOR

This book is aimed at individuals on the autism spectrum who want a self-help guide to improving their happiness and wellbeing, as well as professionals working with individuals on the autism spectrum. Readers who might find this book useful include:

- Individuals on the autism spectrum (including those with Asperger syndrome)
- Autism mentors
- Specialist autism workers
- Adult education tutors and mentors
- University disability officers and mentors
- Speech and language therapists
- Counsellors and therapists

- Health professionals

- Social care professionals

Most of the activities and tasks in this book require a verbal ability to respond and reflect. Therefore, the book is most suited for individuals on the autism spectrum who would traditionally fit the criteria of 'Autism Spectrum Disorder Level 1', 'Asperger syndrome' or 'high-functioning autism', rather than those with significant co-occurring learning and language difficulties.

It is also important not to focus too much on diagnostic labels. Many of these activities have been adapted from strategies that have been shown to be beneficial with the general population. Many individuals can benefit from the suggestions in this book, even if they do not yet have a formal diagnosis of an autism spectrum condition, or do not quite meet formal diagnostic criteria. For that reason, many activities focus more on individuals gaining self-knowledge, rather than focusing on 'stereotypical' autistic traits.

TERMINOLOGY

The terminology used around the autism spectrum is often discussed and much debated. Some individuals prefer identity-first language (*an autistic person*) while others prefer people-first language (*a person with autism*). Some individuals prefer the term 'Asperger syndrome' while others believe that the term 'autistic' better reflects how they interpret and interact with the world.

Diagnostic labels have also changed in recent years. 'Asperger syndrome', 'high-functioning autism', 'pervasive developmental disorder-not otherwise specified (PDD-NOS)' and a range of other diagnoses now all come under the umbrella term of 'the autism spectrum'. Under the newest diagnostic criteria of the *Diagnostic and Statistical Manual of Mental Disorders fifth edition* (*DSM-5*) of the American Psychiatric Association, individuals on the autism spectrum receive a diagnosis of 'Autism Spectrum Disorder Level 1/2/3', depending on the severity of their autism and the impact it has on their daily life.

In this book, for ease of reading, the term 'on the autism spectrum' is used to refer to all individuals on the autism spectrum, including those who identify with the 'Asperger syndrome' or 'high-functioning autism' diagnoses. 'Autism spectrum conditions (ASC)' is used, as opposed to 'autism spectrum disorders (ASD)', to reflect the belief that autism is neither a deficit, disease nor disorder, but simply a different, and equally valid, way of being.

HOW TO USE THIS BOOK

This book is split into sections that can be read independently of each other, although some later activities do build on those earlier in the book. Each chapter begins with a brief introduction to the theory of the topic and its relevance, which is then followed by various ideas for activities and strategies. There are activities to be used by individuals, or by professionals working with individuals, and there are activities designed to be used in group settings.

This book is not designed as a therapeutic intervention to be delivered in a strict order, but more as a collection of strategies and activities to choose from and use when the right opportunity occurs. Although some guidelines have been given as to how you might like to use these activities, they are designed to be flexible and each activity should be adapted to meet individual needs and preferences.

When carrying out the activities in this book, whether as an individual on the autism spectrum or as a professional working with those on the autism spectrum, you might want first to consider the timing and setting. For example:

- Do you have a quiet time and space to work through the activity? Try to find somewhere you are not likely to be interrupted. It can be helpful to turn phones or other devices to 'silent' to reduce interruptions.

- Choose an environment in which you, or the individuals you are supporting, feel comfortable. Where possible, try to reduce any environmental distractions or sensory input.

- Consider the timing. If you or the individuals you are supporting are too tired, you are less likely to be able to concentrate and to think clearly. Equally, feelings of anxiety and frustration can make it difficult to focus on activities that require deeper reflection.

- If you are an individual on the autism spectrum working through this book as a self-help guide, consider where you could get further support, should any issues or concerns arise. You might have a trusted friend or family member, or might have access to a mentor, counsellor, therapist or support worker.

CHAPTER OVERVIEW

Chapter 1, 'If You Only Have Five Minutes...', briefly summarises the main points of this book and signposts readers to key topics and activities.

Chapter 2, 'Understanding the Autism Spectrum' provides an overview of the origins of autism and diagnostic criteria. This chapter also explores some of the common difficulties and differences that individuals on the autism spectrum can experience.

Chapter 3 'Understanding Positive Psychology', discusses the key people and concepts covered by the branch of positive psychology. Some of the main findings of this movement are discussed, as well as the possible benefits of using a positive psychology approach for individuals on the autism spectrum to support them in achieving happiness and wellbeing.

Chapter 4, 'Recognising, Identifying and Using Character Strengths', explores what is meant by 'character strengths' and how we can benefit from recognising and using them. This chapter discusses why individuals who use their character strengths are happier and how this relates to individuals on the autism spectrum.

Chapter 5, 'Cultivating Positive Emotions', identifies various 'positive' emotions and investigates how these can be promoted and cultivated. This chapter reflects on what is meant by happiness. What makes somebody happy? Can happiness be taught? Can we improve our happiness levels? Why can it be difficult for autistic individuals to experience happiness? How to increase hope and optimism is discussed, and the benefits of gratitude and appreciation are considered.

Chapter 6, 'Positive Coping', explores how individuals can learn to cope with some less helpful emotions. This chapter discusses what is meant by resilience and a growth mindset. Why is resilience important and can it be taught? How do we develop resilience? What is meant by a growth mindset and how can this be utilised in the context of autism?

Chapter 7, 'Wellbeing', explains what increases wellbeing levels. Challenges for individuals on the autism spectrum are discussed as well as possible strategies to overcome these.

Chapter 8, 'Meaning, Purpose and Connection', discusses the wider issues. How does having meaning and purpose affect our happiness and wellbeing? What challenges can there be for individuals on the autism spectrum in connecting with others and how can these differences be used positively to increase happiness and wellbeing?

1

IF YOU ONLY HAVE FIVE MINUTES...

WHAT IS AUTISM?

Autism is a spectrum condition that affects people in different ways and with different levels of severity. Some individuals on the autism spectrum may be of average or above-average intelligence, while others may have associated learning difficulties, may require alternative methods of communication and may also need support with everyday living tasks. Autism is a lifelong condition and differences will have been present since childhood. There is no 'cure' for autism, but many adults on the autism spectrum do learn how to cope with and make the most of their differences. With the right support, individuals on the autism spectrum are often able to thrive personally, socially and in employment.

Individuals on the autism spectrum interpret the world differently, connect to others in a different way, and can find other people confusing and unpredictable. The word 'autism' comes from the Greek word '*autos*', meaning 'self'. This reflects the fact that the main difference in individuals on the autism spectrum is how they connect on a social and emotional level with others.

Being on the autism spectrum has been likened to being a computer with a different operating system to the majority – your brain is simply hard-wired a different way. Those on the autism spectrum experience differences in two main areas: social communication and interaction; and restricted and repetitive patterns of behaviours, activities or interests. They might also be over- or under-sensitive to sensory input such as lighting, noise, tastes and touch. Every individual on the autism spectrum is affected slightly differently.

Although autism was traditionally seen as a medical diagnosis – as something 'wrong' with the individual – it is now increasingly being recognised that society has only been designed for one way of being and that it is this that can sometimes have a negative impact on how successful individuals on the autism spectrum are. The concept of neurodiversity is also gaining momentum, with autism, as well as other identified conditions such as dyslexia, dyspraxia and attention deficit hyperactivity disorder (ADHD), increasingly being seen simply as differences in neurological functioning, which should be expected and accepted as part of natural human variation. Within this framework, autism is seen as 'different', not inferior.

WHAT ARE THE DIFFICULTIES?

Living in a world that has not been designed for their ways of thinking, learning and relating to others can be difficult for those on the autism spectrum. Research suggests that individuals on the autism spectrum can be more likely than neurotypicals to experience mental health difficulties such as depression, anxiety and worry. They might also experience lower self-esteem and self-worth, have fewer friendships and relationships, and be more vulnerable to bullying or discrimination. Difficulties or differences with communication can also make interaction difficult. Feeling misunderstood can also be a problem, and unfortunately many autistic individuals report negative experiences of education, employment and community participation. Sometimes individuals on the autism spectrum can be highly qualified and capable, but have difficulty with the social demands of education and the workplace.

INTRODUCING POSITIVE PSYCHOLOGY

Psychology has traditionally focused on the more negative aspects of human life, such as mental illness and disorders. The branch of positive psychology, however, focuses on more positive human experiences such as wellbeing, happiness, human strengths, resilience and flourishing. Positive psychology is the scientific study of these aspects of human existence and is developing a solid evidence base of how to increase and develop these positive experiences and attitudes. Although the field of positive psychology has expanded enormously over the past two decades, relatively little evidence exists about how to apply the findings to individuals on the autism spectrum. This book aims to add to the literature by suggesting challenges and opportunities for individuals on the autism spectrum when using a positive psychology approach.

WHERE TO START IF...

...you are an individual on the autism spectrum:

- Look for the 'individual activities' in each chapter. You can adapt each of these to your individual circumstances and preferences.

- You will also find the 'theory' section of each chapter gives a useful overview of the theory and philosophy behind the activities.

...you are a professional working with people on the autism spectrum on an individual basis:

- Look for the 'individual activities' in each chapter. Adapt these as needed for the individuals you work with.

- The 'group activities' might also be able to be adapted for working with individuals.

- You will find that the 'theory' section of each chapter gives a useful overview of the theory and philosophy behind the activities.

- Read also Chapter 2, 'Understanding the Autism Spectrum', for guidance on working with individuals on the autism spectrum.

...you are a professional working with groups of individuals on the autism spectrum:

- Look for the 'group activities' in each chapter. Adapt these as needed for the groups you work with.

- The 'individual activities' might also be able to be adapted for working with groups.

- You will find that the 'theory' section of each chapter gives a useful overview of the theory and philosophy behind the activities.

- Read also Chapter 2, 'Understanding the Autism Spectrum', for guidance on working with individuals on the autism spectrum.

...you are new to working with people on the autism spectrum:

- Begin with Chapter 2, 'Understanding the Autism Spectrum', for more information about the autism spectrum and working with individuals on the autism spectrum.

- The 'theory' section of each chapter links the activities suggested with the differences experienced by individuals on the autism spectrum.

- Look for the 'group activities' or 'individual activities' depending on your role.

...you do not necessarily have dedicated time with individuals on the autism spectrum but are looking for general strategies you can put into place in your setting:

- Read the chapter Chapter 2, 'Understanding the Autism Spectrum', for general advice and strategies about working with individuals on the autism spectrum.

- Read the 'theory' section of each chapter to gain an overview of some of the difficulties individuals on the autism spectrum can experience.

- Read Chapter 7, 'Wellbeing', for information on creating autism-friendly environments.

2

UNDERSTANDING THE AUTISM SPECTRUM

WHAT DOES 'AUTISM SPECTRUM' MEAN?

Autism spectrum conditions were first identified in the 1940s, although individuals with these characteristics have undoubtedly existed throughout human history. Autism comes from the Greek word '*autos*', meaning 'self'. This reflects the fact that autistic individuals do not connect with other people in the same way as others do. Autistic people can appear quite self-contained, or self-reliant, not connecting instinctively with others. Autism has been described by some as not having the innate capacity to connect on a social level, or having a 'social blindness' (Weldon 2014). Some autistic individuals may feel no desire to connect with other people, while others may wish to but find that they connect differently. Social interaction and social expectations can sometimes appear illogical or unnecessary to individuals on the autism spectrum. Autistic individuals might come across as being 'too honest' or 'too direct' to others.

Autism is not a physical disability, nor is it a mental illness. It is a lifelong neurodevelopmental condition and is currently thought to affect more than 1 in 100 people in the United Kingdom (National Autistic Society 2016a). The exact causes of autism are not yet known, but it is thought to have a genetic basis. Autism is something that individuals are born with; it is not something caused by upbringing or that is developed in later life.

Increasingly, autism is being viewed as a different way of being, rather than a 'disorder'. Being on the autism spectrum has been likened to being a computer with a different operating system to the majority; individuals on the autism spectrum are simply hard-wired differently and so interpret the world in a different way.

Autism is now seen as a 'spectrum' of conditions, with individuals being affected to different degrees. Some individuals on the autism spectrum may be very capable and intelligent in some areas; they might be able to live independently, have professional-level jobs or be experts in their chosen fields. These individuals may have fewer obvious difficulties with language and communication but will still experience significant differences in the way that they connect and relate to others, as well as in how they interpret the world. Other individuals on the autism spectrum may have associated learning difficulties or may be non-verbal, communicating in ways other than using speech. These individuals may need a high level of lifelong care and support. However, all individuals on the autism spectrum share differences in two main areas:

- Social communication and interaction.

- Restricted and repetitive patterns of behaviours, activities or interests (including sensory behaviour).

DIFFICULTIES AND DIFFERENCES EXPERIENCED BY THOSE ON THE AUTISM SPECTRUM
Social communication and interaction

Difficulties or differences can include:

- Feelings of being different and not connecting to others; not having the instinctive ability to 'connect' that others seem to have.

- Interpreting and using verbal language (may have a literal understanding of language, may have difficulty interpreting jokes or sarcasm, may come across as being very 'literal' or too honest, there may be differences in using or understanding tone of voice).

- Interpreting and using non-verbal language (gesture, body language, facial expression).

- Understanding the expectations of conversation (e.g. some individuals might talk at length about their own interests, repeat what the other person has said (echolalia), or have difficulty initiating or ending conversation or staying on topic).

- Following the dynamics of group conversation (such as keeping up with what is being said, knowing when it is your turn to speak or how to interrupt appropriately, processing what others have said).

- Recognising and understanding the thoughts and feelings of other people, and understanding that other people have different beliefs, perspectives and thoughts than their own (also called 'Theory of Mind').

- Recognising, understanding and expressing their own feelings (called 'alexithymia').

- Forming friendships and relationships.

- Appearing different to others (e.g. some might appear 'insensitive' or too direct, may prefer their own company, may not seek comfort from others in typically expected ways or may appear socially inappropriate).

- Feeling overwhelmed by the social world and social interaction.

- Understanding and following social 'norms'.

Restricted and repetitive patterns of behaviours, activities or interests

Difficulties and differences can include:

- Using restricted and repetitive routines to help overcome the difficulties of living in an uncomfortable and unpredictable world (routines can often reduce anxiety).

- Relying on 'rules' (again, rules can make an unpredictable and confusing world, appear more predictable and clear; therefore, when 'rules' or expectations are applied inconsistently, some individuals on the autism spectrum can feel very insecure and frustrated).

- Finding it difficult to cope with change or new experiences.

- Having intense and highly focused interests (often called 'special interests').

- Sensory processing differences (see below).

Sensory differences

It is increasingly recognised that many individuals on the autism spectrum also experience sensory difficulties. Individuals may be hypo- (under-) or hyper- (over-) sensitive to various sensory inputs.

EXAMPLES OF SENSORY DIFFERENCES

Vision

Under-sensitive: Enjoys bright lights and movement; objects appear dark or lose their features. Objects appear blurred.

Over-sensitive: Prefers dimmer light, overwhelmed by too much light (especially fluorescent lighting), complex patterns or too many visual distractions.

Sound

Under-sensitive: Might only hear certain sounds, or sounds in one ear. Might like loud noises.

Over-sensitive: Noise can appear amplified (a loud voice can be interpreted as shouting, the hum of a computer can be overwhelming). Difficulties in eliminating background noise and being able to concentrate on a conversation.

Smell
Under-sensitive: May have no sense of smell and fail to identify smells (including their own body odour).

Over-sensitive: Smells can be intense and overpowering. May dislike people wearing certain perfumes or deodorants.

Taste
Under-sensitive: May like very spicy food or may eat everything (e.g. soil, grass, play dough).

Over-sensitive: Finds some foods and flavours overpowering due to sensitive taste buds. Certain textures cause discomfort.

Touch
Under-sensitive: Needs to hold others tightly before there is a sensation of having applied any pressure. High pain threshold. Enjoys heavy objects on top of them (e.g. weighted blankets).

Over-sensitive: Touch can be painful – may have a strong dislike of other people touching them. May dislike having things on hands, feet or head. Some fabrics can feel painful or 'scratchy'.

Vestibular system
The vestibular system helps us to maintain balance and tells us how fast our body is moving.

Under-sensitive: May need to rock, swing or spin.

Over-sensitive: May have difficulty with controlling body movement or car sickness.

Proprioception
Proprioception is our body awareness system, which integrates information about the position and movement of our body in space. Difficulties for individuals on the autism spectrum may include standing too close to people, standing too far away, bumping into things, needing to lean on things, or difficulty with fine motor skills.

Differences between males and females on the autism spectrum

Traditionally, autism was considered by many to be a 'male' condition, and many more males were diagnosed than females. Participants in the original autism research of the 1940s had mainly been male, and diagnostic criteria had developed out of this. Media portrayals of autism have also generally reflected these male presentations of autism (e.g. in the film *Rain Man* and Mark Haddon's novel *The Curious Incident of the Dog in the Night-Time*). It is now recognised, however, that just as many females may be affected by autism as males. The difference is that they might often cope with their autism differently, making the autism harder to identify. There is currently much research going on in this area, but some possible differences identified so far include the following:

- Females on the autism spectrum are more likely to 'mask', hide or camouflage their difficulties. They might be more able to copy and mimic others, hiding some of their difficulties with social interaction (Hurley 2014). Their differences may, therefore, be less obvious to observers.

- Males may respond to their difficulties with more challenging behaviour (Hurley 2014), while females may internalise their difficulties (Soloman *et al.* 2012), leading to mental health difficulties such as depression or anxiety. Again, difficulties may be less noticed.

- Females on the autism spectrum may show less restricted and repetitive patterns of behaviour than males on the autism spectrum (Van Wijngaarden *et al.* 2014).

- Whereas males may have special interests that are unusual and stand out, females' special interests may be similar to those of their neurotypical peers; the difference is the intensity and dominance of these interests (Gould and Ashton-Smith 2011).

- Girls and women on the autism spectrum may develop 'coping strategies' that hide their difficulties (Attwood 2007).

- Females on the autism spectrum may be more open to talking about their feelings and may be more expressive in gesture, tone of voice and facial expression than males on the autism spectrum (Simone, 2010).

- Females on the autism spectrum without co-occurring learning difficulties might be particularly hard to identify, meaning they might have missed out on support when younger.

TIP! Remember that the central characteristics of autism are still the same in males and females (i.e. there will still be significant differences in social communication and interaction); it is simply how some females may cope with these difficulties that is different.

Difficulties for adults on the autism spectrum

No two individuals on the autism spectrum will experience the same differences and difficulties. Autism is a very individual condition and is seen as a spectrum. Therefore, it is impossible to identify and list every difficulty or challenge that individuals on the autism spectrum might face. It is important, also, to recognise that environments and other people can influence how well an individual on the autism spectrum copes from day to day. However, some difficulties that can commonly occur include:

- Differences in learning styles (meaning academic potential might not have been recognised or realised).

- Difficulties with the social aspects of college or university, leading to courses not having been completed.

- Finding the social aspects of the workplace difficult.

- Finding it difficult to gain employment due to difficulties in applying for jobs or performing well at interviews.

- Difficulties with 'office politics' or connecting with colleagues.

- Finding it difficult to find a work environment that suits them.

- Being over-qualified for the role they find themselves in, leading to frustration.

- Sometimes preferring to work alone or in a quiet environment.

- Making and maintaining friendships.

- Making and maintaining intimate relationships.

- Perhaps not enjoying socialising in 'typical' ways.

- Needing more time alone than others.

- Finding socialising and the social interaction of the workplace exhausting, and therefore needing time to 'recover'.

- Feelings of being different to others.

- Being discriminated against or bullied.

- Feelings of isolation and loneliness.

- Low self-esteem and self-worth, perhaps lacking confidence to try new things or put themselves forward.

- Finding it difficult to communicate and feeling misunderstood.

- Experiencing frequent misunderstandings or communication breakdowns.

- Experiencing discomfort in certain environments due to sensory inputs.

- Lacking a supportive network of people around them.

- Finding it difficult to identify and understand their feelings.

- Finding it difficult to find others with similar interests and values.

- Difficulties in expressing their needs and perspectives to others, including professionals.

- Trying too hard to 'fit in' and becoming exhausted by this.

- Not having the access to the support needed.

AN AUTISM DIAGNOSIS

Autism is usually diagnosed by a multi-disciplinary team, often made up of psychiatrists, psychologists and other health professionals. Many professionals use the *DSM-5* to diagnose. This latest (2013) edition of the American Psychiatric Association's manual has removed some terms that were given in the past as separate diagnoses (e.g. 'Asperger syndrome', 'high-functioning autism' and 'PDD-NOS'). Individuals are now all given a diagnosis of 'autism spectrum disorder' on a sliding scale of 'severity', depending on how far the condition impacts on everyday life for the individual in question:

Autism Spectrum Disorder Level 1: Requiring support (individuals with 'Asperger syndrome' would usually fit this category)

Autism Spectrum Disorder Level 2: Requiring significant support

Autism Spectrum Disorder Level 3: Requiring very substantial support

Autism can occur with or without additional conditions and disabilities. Other difficulties that can also often occur in individuals on the autism spectrum can include conditions such as general learning difficulties, ADHD, dyslexia, or dyspraxia.

NEURODIVERSITY AND OTHER THEORIES

There are different ways of viewing autism. Some view it as a 'disorder', as something 'inferior', whereas others see if simply as a different way of being, one equally as valid as any other way of being.

Models of disability

Using the *medical model* of disability, autism is classed as a 'disorder', something wrong within the individual that needs to be treated, 'fixed' or cured, in order to make that individual more 'normal'. A *social model* of disability, however, implies that individuals are only disabled by the society around them, that environments, policies and practices put some individuals (such as those on the autism spectrum) at a disadvantage; it is society that needs to change to become more inclusive. An alternative paradigm – that of *neurodiversity* – is also gaining in popularity.

KEY TERMS

Neurodiversity: The diversity of ways in which humans think, learn and relate to others (in the same way as we have cultural diversity, gender diversity or biodiversity).

The neurodiversity paradigm: The neurodiversity paradigm views these differences in neurocognitive functioning as a normal, and totally expected, part of human variation. No one way of functioning is considered to be superior to any other.

This book uses the neurodiversity paradigm as the underpinning theoretical approach. The autistic way of being is not considered inferior to any other way, nor is it seen as something that needs to be fixed. This is not a book about making individuals on the autism spectrum more 'normal'; rather it is about helping them to be happy and confident to be themselves, and helping them and others to believe that their way of being is just as 'normal' as anybody else's. There is also a focus on changing attitudes of other people and of society in general to be more accepting of the wonderful diversity of human life.

COMMUNICATING WITH INDIVIDUALS ON THE AUTISM SPECTRUM

Do not assume that every individual on the autism spectrum needs, or wants, to be supported in the same way. If you are a professional working with individuals on the autism spectrum, the best thing you can do is to get to know the individuals you are working with. Find out how individuals like to communicate and what works best for them. Some general principles include:

- **Use a calm, neutral tone of voice.** Some individuals on the autism spectrum can be highly sensitive to sound. A loud voice might be interpreted as angry or shouting.

- **Use fewer words.** Some individuals on the autism spectrum can find it difficult to filter out what is important and what is not. Stick to the key points and state these clearly.

- **Use social 'chit-chat' carefully.** Some individuals on the autism spectrum can find this sort of communication difficult and might be better communicating when there is a clear purpose.

- **Mean what you say and say what you mean.** Try to be as honest and as clear as possible. Explain if you change your mind, get something wrong or if circumstances change.

- **Use visual support to aid understanding.** Examples could include timetables, flow charts or diagrams.

- **Explain any non-literal language that may be new to the individual you are communicating with.** Such language might include idioms, metaphors, sarcasm, jokes or regional expressions.

- **Remove background noise and talk in a quiet environment.** Some individuals on the autism spectrum can find it difficult to filter out background noise and this can increase anxiety levels.

- **Keep language clear and simple.** Sometimes professionals can use specific vocabulary that might be new for some individuals. Remember, too, that each person will have a different amount of prior knowledge about autism and how it affects them.

- **Allow time to process.** Don't be afraid of waiting and of silence in conversation. Some individuals need this time to make sense of what they are hearing and to formulate their response. Some individuals might appear as if they are unable to 'let go' or to 'forget' about things. Sometimes this might simply be because they have needed longer to process their emotions and feelings about an event than other people and were not able to reflect at the time.

- **See if communicating on a one-to-one basis makes a difference.** Some individuals on the autism spectrum find it easier to communicate one-to-one rather than in a larger group.

- **Find out individuals' preferred methods of communication.** Some prefer to communicate via email or writing rather than in person. Others might find telephone conversations particularly difficult.

- **Be aware that some individuals on the autism spectrum find eye contact uncomfortable.** This does not mean they are not listening.

- **Try not to mislabel the feelings of those on the autism spectrum.** Show acceptance for the fact that their ways of interpreting the world, and their preferences, are equally as valid as anybody else's. Try not to tell an individual how they should or should not be feeling in a particular situation.

- **Avoid 'jumping in' and talking on behalf of an individual on the autism spectrum** or 'putting words into their mouth'.

- **Give forewarning.** Let individuals on the autism spectrum know what is coming up and about any changes to routine.

- **Do what you say you will do.** If you promise to get some information for an individual or to get back to them, make sure that you do, or let them know that you won't be able to.

Active listening

It is important to listen and respond to individuals on the autism spectrum in an open and non-judgemental manner. One method of doing this is 'active listening'. The concept of active listening is often referred to in counselling and psychotherapy, but it is a useful strategy for anybody to use to improve their listening skills.

- **Show that you are listening.** Be aware of any messages that your body language might be giving. Ensure that your facial expression, posture and gestures are open and relaxed.

- **Avoid distractions in the environment.** Fidgeting, looking at your watch or clock, glancing at your phone, and typing while talking are all actions that suggest to the speaker that your focus is not on them.

- **Be mindful of distracting thoughts.** Try to avoid any internal distractions of your own so that you can really focus on what the individual is saying Make a mental note if you feel your attention wandering (e.g. 'What's for dinner this evening? I really must call into the grocery store on my way home.'), and bring your attention back to the present moment. It can be very easy to let our thoughts wander when listening, and before we know it, we have lost track of what is being said.

- **Try not to plan your response while the person is speaking.** Try instead to focus carefully on the words that are being used. If you are planning what you are going to say next, your attention is not completely on what is being said.

- **Ask questions to clarify points.** If you really have not understood, then do not pretend to. Be honest and ask the other person to repeat what they said to you, or ask them if they could help you to understand by explaining further.

- **Avoid using 'why'.** Too many 'why' questions can begin to sound like an interrogation. 'Why' questions can also be perceived at times to be blaming or criticising. Use other question words or use comments rather than questions to avoid the conversation sounding like an interrogation.

- **Use a calm and neutral tone of voice.** This is especially important when working with individuals on the autism spectrum as many can have heightened sensory sensitivities, or can have difficulty in interpreting tone of voice. Speaking in a loud voice, for example, may come across as shouting or being angry. 'Over-enthusiasm' could be perceived as being 'fake' or patronising.

- **Accept what is said without commenting, judging or criticising.** This can be difficult, especially if you have strong opinions of your own or if you believe the other person is wrong. Remember, you do not have to agree with the other person inside; just try to avoid any intentional, or unintentional, judgement or criticism.

- **Avoid asking leading questions.** Try not to put words into the other person's mouth. Questions such as 'And then what happened – you went to report the accident to your supervisor?' invite the individual to agree, as do questions such as 'Being alone is so boring, isn't it?'

- **Occasionally reflect back what the speaker is saying, or summarise the main points.** Try to use the speaker's own words when possible.

3

UNDERSTANDING POSITIVE PSYCHOLOGY

WHAT IS POSITIVE PSYCHOLOGY?

The discipline of psychology has traditionally focused on deficits, difficulties and disorders, examining the more negative aspects of human life. For many people, the term 'psychology' is synonymous with mental illness, and psychologists are those tasked with understanding and curing these 'diseases and disorders'.

However, since the turn of the 21st century a new movement, 'positive psychology' has been gathering momentum. Rather than delving into negatives and 'What's gone wrong?', positive psychology instead investigates the more positive aspects of human existence – positive emotions; human resourcefulness and resilience; strengths; talents and flourishing – all at both an individual and collective level. In the words of the movement's founder, Martin Seligman, positive psychology is summarised as the 'scientific study of optimal human functioning that aims to discover and promote the factors that allow individuals and communities to thrive' (Seligman and Csikszentmihalyi 2000, p.5).

KEY PEOPLE

Martin Seligman: Psychologist seen as the 'founder' of the positive psychology movement.

Mikhail Csikszentmihalyi: A key positive psychologist who named and explored the theory of 'flow' – total engagement in an activity that brings intrinsic enjoyment.

Positive psychology is now a rapidly expanding field and aims to bring solid, scientific, empirical research evidence to the study of happiness and wellbeing. Many ideas from positive psychology are beginning to move into mainstream culture; governments and other large organisations are using findings from the movement to influence policy and practice.

WHAT DOES POSITIVE PSYCHOLOGY COVER?

- Positive emotions
- Happiness
- Life satisfaction
- Wellbeing
- Optimism
- Hope
- Creativity
- Flow
- Strengths and virtues
- Wisdom
- Courage
- Emotional intelligence

- Self-esteem
- Positive coping
- Resilience
- Motivation
- Achieving goals
- Coaching
- Positive relationships
- Positive therapy
- Positive education
- Wellbeing at work
- Positive parenting

WHAT HAS POSITIVE PSYCHOLOGY TOLD US SO FAR?

Positive psychology as a discipline has developed quickly and new findings are constantly being added to the body of knowledge. Go into any large bookstore and you will find rows of books on related topics. Some of the main findings so far have suggested:

- Happiness levels tend to decrease in middle life, with people in their 20s and 60s being happier than those in-between (Office for National Statistics 2016).

- Being grateful and experiencing feelings of gratitude tends to increase happiness (Emmons 2007; Lyubomirsky 2007).

- Positive emotional states can have a positive impact on physical health (Boniwell and Ryan 2012).

- People who perceive themselves as having good physical health are happier than those who perceive themselves as being in poor health (Office for National Statistics 2016).

- Money does not seem to increase happiness as much as enjoying your job or having a supportive social network (Easterlin 2008).

- Using our strengths can increase feelings of happiness and wellbeing (Boniwell 2015).

- 'Flow' is a positive emotional state that increases wellbeing (Csikszentmihalyi 1992).

- Resilience and a growth mindset can be developed in individuals (Dweck 2006).

Positive psychologists have also identified ten 'keys' to happier living (Rae 2016). These are ten scientifically proven things that can increase happiness levels. They make the acronym 'GREAT DREAM'.

Giving – Doing things for others, donating our time, ideas and energy. Helping others makes the 'helper' feel good too.

Relating – Connecting with other people. People with strong social relationships are happier and healthier.

Exercise – Being active increases happiness and improves our mood.

Appreciating – Appreciating and taking notice of the world around us helps us to feel better.

Trying out – Learning new things helps us to stay curious and engaged, whether through formal learning, hobbies or learning new skills.

Direction – Having goals to look forward to can motivate us and helps us to feel good about the future.

Resilience – 'Bouncing back' and how we respond to negative situations has an impact on our wellbeing.

Emotion – Experiencing positive emotions such as joy, gratitude, contentment and inspiration improves wellbeing, as does having a positive attitude.

Acceptance – Accepting ourselves and not comparing ourselves to others increase feelings of happiness.

Meaning – Being part of something bigger and having meaning and purpose in our life help us to feel happier, more in control and more purposeful.

Even just reading these you may already be identifying some reasons why individuals on the autism spectrum can find it harder to feel a sense of happiness and wellbeing. For example, individuals on the autism spectrum might not desire or have strong social connections, and might have often been negatively compared to others. You will learn more throughout this book about possible challenges for those on the autism spectrum and how to overcome them.

REMEMBER! This is a very brief overview. Look at the 'Further Reading and Resources' section at the end of this book if you are interested in finding out more.

POSITIVE PSYCHOLOGY AS A MAINSTREAM MOVEMENT

Findings from the positive psychology movement are rapidly entering popular culture and mainstream organisations. In fact, barely a day goes by without the popular media containing some mention of how we can improve our happiness or wellbeing. So, where has this interest come from?

Until the end of the 20th century, psychology was focused mainly on remediating diseases and disorders, on getting people back to a 'normal' level of functioning. Psychologists examined medical disorders, and a trip to the psychologist would have usually had negative associations – there must be something very 'wrong' with you. However, the last century was a time of huge change in most economically developed countries. Most of us no longer have to worry about having enough food to eat or finding shelter. We have access to education, health and care services. Now that our basic needs have been met, the focus of our attention has shifted – we now no longer have to worry about survival, so can think instead about improving our levels of happiness and wellbeing.

In addition, the overt consumerism of the later 20th century has contributed to changing attitudes. The myth was previously perpetuated that wealth would bring happiness and we should strive for a higher income, our own house, cars and other possessions as these would improve our levels of wellbeing. This general view has shifted in recent years, with society having almost reached saturation point when it comes to material possessions. Many people are realising that despite this material wealth and feelings of security, they still feel unhappy and unfulfilled.

The rapid increase in mental health difficulties in society is leading individuals, professionals and large organisations to look for ways of promoting happiness and wellbeing. Positive psychology is not about treating mental illness but more about helping anybody increase their happiness, improve their wellbeing and develop positive ways of coping.

The world is recognising the importance of happiness and wellbeing, and how this is fundamental to other forms of success, rather than the other way around. Bhutan, for example, is often cited as being the happiest country in the world, despite having a range of social and economic problems. The country introduced 'Gross National Happiness' as a scheme in 1978 and, since then, life expectancy has increased by 20 years and household income per capita by 450 per cent (Blyth 2013), demonstrating that focusing on happiness can impact positively on many other aspects of life.

THE BENEFITS OF USING POSITIVE PSYCHOLOGY AS AN APPROACH

Just as within the general population, emotional wellbeing and happiness have traditionally received little attention in the field of autism studies. Most interventions for autistic individuals have instead considered success criteria as increases in adaptive functioning (e.g. getting a job, needing less support, living independently, having friends, or reducing social 'unacceptable' behaviour). It is now recognised that the assumption that these things will automatically bring happiness and thriving for autistic people needs to be challenged (Vermeulen 2014). It does not follow that an autistic individual who lives independently will be happier, just as it should not be assumed that an individual who needs a high level of support will be unhappy.

Indeed, there is, in fact, little evidence that improving outcomes such as level of independence or social skills also improves happiness levels in autistic individuals. Some evidence suggests that the 'severity' of a person's autism has far less impact on wellbeing levels than the discrepancy between their needed and received support (Renty and Roeyers 2006). So whatever the level of an individual's needs, if they feel they are receiving the necessary support for these, they will be happier than if they feel they are not receiving the support they need. Other studies have indicated that greater perceived support from family and friends is associated with a better quality of life for autistic individuals (Khanna *et al.* 2014) and that quality of life in autistic individuals was found to correlate with taking part in regular and meaningful recreational activities, rather than being related to their occupation, intelligence or housing situation (Billstedt, Gillberg and Gillberg 2011).

There is no doubt that traditional measures of success are important – academic achievement can mean greater access to jobs, having a job can increase feelings of confidence and competence, and improving social skills can reduce the anxiety and misunderstandings that come with social interaction – however, it should not be assumed that these things alone will improve happiness and wellbeing.

Individuals on the autism spectrum can also be more likely than others to experience mental health difficulties such as depression and anxiety (Van Heijst and Geurts 2014). Some of the reasons for this are discussed later in this book, but it is perhaps inevitable that individuals who experience difficulties with social interaction and find the world to be a confusing and unpredictable place will experience feelings of loneliness, isolation, uncertainty and depression. It is another reason to help individuals on the autism spectrum to improve their happiness and wellbeing levels.

Many positive psychology interventions have not yet been trialled or adapted for individuals on the autism spectrum. That's why this book has been written – there are specific issues to take into account when working with individuals on the autism spectrum, and some approaches designed for non-autistic people may not be helpful to those on the autism spectrum.

This book adapts some evidence-based positive psychology interventions for autism. Professionals need to be aware of using traditional questionnaires and surveys designed for the neurotypical population with individuals on the autism spectrum as there can be differences in communication and in how questions are interpreted. Furthermore, it is also important to remember that what makes neurotypical people happy may not also make autistic people happy. As Vermeulen (2014) says: 'We should avoid forcing autistic people into a neurotypical concept of happiness; happiness is a personal and subjective construct and the things that make an autistic person happy do not necessarily mirror those that make a neurotypical person happy'.

Positive psychology or positive thinking

Positive psychology is not the same as positive thinking. Having a positive attitude does help, and some aspects of positive psychology do focus on helping individuals and organisations to develop this, but positive psychology is based on scientific evidence as to what has been proven to be helpful. Positive psychology is 'positive' in that it is concerned with developing the positive things in life, such as human strengths, beneficial emotions, wellbeing, resilience and flourishing. Positive thinking alone does not encourage the actions that are necessary for lasting change to take place.

Positive psychology and mindfulness

Over the past decade, the awareness and popularity of mindfulness have grown enormously. Mindfulness has been associated with many benefits, such as increasing happiness and wellbeing, improving mental health conditions and treating many other physical and psychological complaints. Mindfulness has its origins in Buddhist traditions and simply means paying attention to the present moment, and observing thoughts and feelings non-judgementally, without engaging with them. Mindfulness has been adapted for the Western mindset in recent years, with many people using mindfulness apps, or attending courses and workshops.

Mindfulness is often association with observing and accepting an event, situation, thought or feeling, rather than struggling with it and trying to change it. Witnessing experiences with interest and kindness towards yourself can limit the impact of more negative thoughts and feelings.

In his book *Hardwiring Happiness*, Rick Hanson discusses how working with your mind (such as when using positive psychology approaches) is not at odds with mindfulness:

> Merely witnessing stress, worries, irritability or a blue mood will not uproot any of these... Nor does being with your mind by itself grow gratitude, enthusiasm, honesty, creativity or many other strengths... You need to work with your mind to build up the inner strength of mindfulness. (Hanson 2013, p.8)

Limitations of positive psychology

Every approach has its limitations. Critics of the positive psychology approach would claim that positive psychology focuses too much on cultivating happy and pleasurable feelings, while demonising sad or painful feelings (Baylis 2009), thus giving unrealistic expectations and dismissing the full, and necessary, spectrum of human feelings. Other criticisms include the view that psychological approaches prioritise thinking, rather than taking a more holistic approach bringing together mind, body, soul and our environments (Baylis 2009).

Approaches outlined in this book

This book uses a number of strategies in conjunction with positive psychology approaches. Imagine a bad storm comes to your town. At the time, the safest and most beneficial course of action might be to stay inside and simply observe from the window. Going out and fighting against gale-force winds is unlikely to be successful. Worrying needlessly will also not change the outcome. Once the storm has passed, however, the time might be right to go outside and remove some of the fallen roof tiles, branches and debris. You might also decide to future-proof your garden – by replacing broken fence panels with more secure ones, for example – and you might reflect on the positives or lessons learned. It's the same with your mind – there are times when observing with acceptance might be the best thing to do; at other times, strengthening positive neural pathways, or replacing less helpful ones, will be more useful.

There are times when acceptance of neurodiversity and difference will be most helpful – on the part of both autistic and neurotypical individuals. Simply accepting that brains and people are different, and not placing judgements on these differences, will go a long way to reducing stigma and making the world an easier place for neurodivergent individuals to live in. It is also helpful for individuals on the autism spectrum to empower themselves to thrive in this imperfect world by building up a clear picture of their strengths, understanding what makes them happy and increasing their ability to respond with resilience.

Finally, this book also recognises that human minds do not exist in isolation – we are influenced by the environments around us and our physical bodies.

4

RECOGNISING, IDENTIFYING AND USING CHARACTER STRENGTHS

CHARACTER STRENGTHS: THE THEORY

This chapter looks at character strengths and the benefits of identifying, recognising and utilising these. It is often hard to identify our strengths. Many of us find it easy to be critical about ourselves, but more difficult to show ourselves kindness and compassion.

KEY TERMS

What is the difference between character strengths, skills, gifts and talents?

Character strengths: Character strengths are generally considered to be positive character traits used across various aspects of our personal, educational, social or vocational lives. Examples of character strengths are creativity, gratitude, perseverance, teamwork, and appreciation of beauty.

Skills: A skill is usually considered to be an acquired ability or expertise that has required training or practice. Skills can be 'hard' skills (e.g. computer skills, reading, budgeting and gardening) or 'soft' skills, which are harder to measure (e.g. listening, friendship and communication skills).

Gifts and talents: A 'gift' or 'talent' is usually considered to be an innate aptitude in a certain area; for example, we often talk about people being gifted in music, art or sport.

The importance of recognising and using our strengths

The concept of identifying and developing strengths is central to positive psychology. But why is it so important to be able to recognise our strengths? Research suggests that there are many links between strengths, wellbeing and life satisfaction:

- Recognising and following our strengths generates optimism (Boniwell 2008).

- Using our strengths feels authentic and energising (Linley 2008).

- Knowledge of our strengths helps to bring a sense of fulfilment and helps us to achieve our goals (Boniwell 2008; Linley et al. 2010).

- Top achievers have been shown to build their lives around their talents and strengths, while recognising, understanding and managing their weaknesses (Clifton and Anderson 2001).

- Adolescents' knowledge and development of their strengths has a positive effect on preventing negative outcomes and indicates positive development and thriving (Park and Peterson 2006).

- People who use their strengths more have higher levels of self-efficacy (Govindji and Linley 2007) and self-esteem (Minhas 2010).

- Putting our strengths to work on a daily basis can have a lasting positive effect on our happiness levels (Boniwell 2015).

- Using our core strengths means we are likely to feel more confident, less stressed and are more likely to achieve our goals (King 2015).

- Further evidence suggests that strengths-based interventions can have lasting effects on young people (Wilson 2011) as they then develop a more positive view of themselves, which can lead to sustained change.

Focusing on strengths does not mean blindly overlooking any weaknesses; ignoring these could lead to an unrealistic sense of self. Positive psychology instead advocates working towards strengths and finding new ways to apply these in our life, while at the same time recognising our lower strengths and using our top strengths to manage and develop these. It is also important to note that in some studies the positive effects of using strengths only endured if participants were told to use a chosen strength in a new and different way each day, rather than if they were just told to use their strengths more (Seligman *et al.* 2005). Therefore, it is not only important for individuals to recognise their strengths but also to learn how to put these to use in various contexts.

Strengths are not fixed but continue to develop over time. Some evidence suggests that, on average, about one-third of a person's strengths are innate, whereas the other two-thirds are improved over time – they can be learned and cultivated (Hanson 2013).

How are strengths classified?

We know why identifying our strengths is important, but just what exactly counts as a strength?

Strengths have been classified in different ways. Perhaps the best known is the VIA Character Survey, which identifies 24 different strengths, split into six different categories. A further classification system, Gallup's StrengthsFinder, identifies 34 different strengths, and other systems recognise different numbers and types of strengths. Generally, all classification systems consider strengths to be traits that are considered positive across different cultures and societies.

SOME COMMONLY IDENTIFIED STRENGTHS

Adaptability, Appreciation of beauty, Authenticity, Bravery, Creativity, Critical thinking, Curiosity, Emotional intelligence, Enthusiasm, Equality, Fairness, Forgiveness, Generosity, Gratitude, Honesty, Hope, Humour, Integrity, Justice, Kindness, Leadership, Love of learning, Loving, Modesty, Open-mindedness, Optimism, Organisation, Originality, Patience, Perseverance, Perspective, Prudence, Relationships, Responsibility, Self-awareness, Self-control, Social intelligence, Spirituality, Teamwork, Vitality, Wisdom.

The strengths that an individual possesses the most are often called their 'signature strengths'. These are the strengths that, when we use and cultivate them, help us to feel authentic and energised. So, for example, somebody who would consider a 'love of learning' as their signature strength is likely to feel vibrant and fulfilled when working in a job that involves gaining new knowledge, when researching a new hobby, or when finding out about a new holiday destination. The same person may feel bored and unfulfilled when in a repetitive, monotonous job with no opportunities for new learning. Knowledge of our strengths can help us to seek out situations that fulfil us, rather than ones that are less meaningful to us.

Strengths and individuals on the autism spectrum

It can be beneficial for us all to be able to recognise our signature strengths; this awareness improves not only our self-esteem and confidence, but also helps us to reach our goals and to make more effective decisions relating to our education, employment, relationships and personal life. So why is this knowledge particularly important to develop in individuals on the autism spectrum?

- Recognising strengths is a good way for individuals to start to identify their positive qualities and what is good about themselves, rather than focusing on what is different, difficult or negative.

- Many people, whether they are on the autism spectrum or not, are afraid to be their authentic self. Many people 'wear a mask' to cover up their true feelings and worry how to behave; only on dropping this mask can we become true to ourselves and accept ourselves for who we are (Kaufman 1991). This has particular poignancy for individuals on the autism spectrum.

- Research suggests that children and young people on the autism spectrum can have lower self-esteem and self-worth than their more typically developing peers (Jamison and Schuttler 2015). There are several explanations for this: young people on the autism spectrum may experience direct, and indirect, comparisons to their peers; they may receive negative reactions from others; they may feel 'odd', 'different' or 'wrong'; and they may feel that it is not OK to be themselves. These feelings can then continue into adulthood.

- Some individuals on the autism spectrum, perhaps particularly females, can also lack a secure sense of self-identity (Simone 2010). This could be because they try hard to copy or mimic others in order to 'fit in', perhaps try to hide aspects of themselves that they consider to be less acceptable, or perhaps have fewer opportunities and interactions with others that allow them to develop a sense of self and individuality.

- Individuals on the autism spectrum may find that they often end up focusing on their perceived 'weaknesses' or areas they need to improve on. Targets set when at school, college or university may focus on comparing individuals with neurotypical expectations, rather than on what they already do well. This emphasis can lead to an unbalanced focus on the 'negatives'.

- Individuals on the autism spectrum may have strengths that have never been recognised as such, and therefore perceive them as negatives. Take a person who has an intense hyperfocus and perseverance with a special interest, for example. Instead of this being recognised as a strength, the individual might have been told that they are selfish for not participating in family life, or 'odd' for not pursuing more typical leisure pursuits. Equally, a person who quickly identifies inconsistencies and discrepancies may be told that they are being pedantic or facetious, when such an ability would be highly sought after in careers such as the law or academia.

- Evidence also suggests that children and young people on the autism spectrum are more likely to experience mental health difficulties, including depression, anxiety and obsessive-compulsive disorder (Kim *et al.* 2000). Research on the value of knowing and following your strengths indicates that this can generate optimism, confidence and bring a sense of fulfilment (Boniwell 2008) and so can support positive mental wellbeing.

In the autism literature you might come across lists of 'autistic strengths'. These often include characteristics such as:

- Specialist knowledge of topics of interest

- Excellent memory for facts and figures

- High motivation for special interests

- Accuracy

- Attention to detail

- Following instructions precisely

- Seeing the world from a different perspective

- Innovative

- Honest

- Non-judgemental

- Sense of loyalty

- Unique sense of humour

- Logical

- Less concern for what others think

- Independent

- Sticking to routines

- Enjoying their own company

Many of these things are strengths for individuals on the autism spectrum, but do not be limited by such stereotypical lists – autistic individuals are as varied as their non-autistic counterparts.

CHARACTER STRENGTHS: PUTTING IT INTO PRACTICE
Individual activities

The following activities are designed for individuals on the autism spectrum to work through independently. There is no 'right way' to complete these activities. You might like to write, draw, type, make a collage or simply think about your answers. Professionals working on a one-to-one basis with individuals on the autism spectrum might also like to guide their clients through these activities. Many can be used as a starting point for further discussion and deeper exploration.

FIND YOUR STRENGTHS

Aim: To support you in recognising and identifying your strengths.

STRENGTHS

- Adaptability
- Appreciation of beauty
- Authenticity
- Bravery
- Creativity
- Critical thinking
- Curiosity
- Emotional intelligence
- Enthusiasm
- Equality
- Fairness
- Forgiveness
- Generosity
- Gratitude
- Honesty
- Hope
- Humour
- Integrity
- Justice
- Kindness
- Leadership
- Love of learning
- Loving
- Modesty
- Open-mindedness
- Optimism
- Organisation
- Originality
- Patience
- Perseverance
- Perspective
- Prudence
- Relationships
- Responsibility
- Self-awareness
- Self-control
- Social intelligence
- Spirituality
- Teamwork
- Vitality
- Wisdom

How to do it:

1. Look at the list of strengths. Pick five or six that you think are your top strengths. For each one identify several examples of when you have used this strength. Example (love of learning):

    'I enjoy researching new topics that I encounter.'

2. If you find this difficult, you could try asking trusted friends or family what they think your strengths are.

3. A further idea is to 'collect' your strengths over a period of time. Every day, write down things that have gone well and which strength you demonstrated. After a few weeks you will have a list of strengths you are using frequently. Example (perseverance):

    'I went back to taekwondo this week, even though I have been finding it difficult during the past few sessions.'

4. You could also try using an online strengths quiz (such as viacharacter.org) in which you answer questions about yourself. The results are then processed to demonstrate your top strengths. Be aware that these sorts of surveys are never completely accurate as they require self-evaluation and a degree of honesty. When completing any survey, it can be easy to answer about the person we would like to be, or the person we think we should be, rather than our true self.

5. Use a combination of these ideas to help you identify your top strengths. Remember that our strengths can change and develop as we go through life, so come back to this activity in the future.

REFRAMING 'NEGATIVE' TRAITS

Aim: To identify the strengths in what you or others might have previously identified as 'negative' traits.

How to do it: As humans, we often have a 'negativity bias', meaning we focus more on the negatives rather than the positives. We might find ourselves focusing on negative things others have said about us, instead of realising that their opinions are just that – opinions. Opinions are not the truth and represent only one person's perspective. However, it can be easy to take these things to heart. Try this activity to build a more balanced view.

1. Consider whether there are any words others have used to describe you that you feel are more negative.

2. Now try reframing these so that you identify the positive. Examples:

   'A past colleague said that I was pedantic, but this just shows I have good attention to detail and notice things that others do not.'

   'I have been told that I am not very sociable, but this shows that I enjoy my own company and am confident doing things independently.'

3. Doing this activity, you might realise that you identify more of your strengths and can add them to your list.

CULTIVATING TOP STRENGTHS

Aim: To identify opportunities to use and develop your top strengths, particularly to support your lower strengths.

How to do it: Identifying our strengths can be useful, but experts suggest that we benefit most when we put our strengths to good use on a daily basis. When we are using our strengths we are likely to feel more fulfilled and confident.

1. Identify your top three or four strengths, using the previous two activities.

2. Now consider whether there are any opportunities in your week for you to use these strengths in new and different ways. Examples:

   'One of my strengths is appreciation of beauty. I could go and look around the art gallery after work one evening. I could also go for a walk in the forest at the weekend as I know the bluebells are beautiful at this time of year.'

   'One of my strengths is organisation. I do some volunteer work at a charity shop and there is a cupboard full of unsorted donations. I could offer to sort and catalogue the cupboard so that all members of staff know what we have.'

3. Next, consider some of your lower strengths that you might like to improve. Consider how you could use some of your top strengths to develop these. Example:

   'I am not always very optimistic about things that are going to happen. I focus on what could go wrong. However, one of my top strengths is organisation, so I will use this to help me. Instead of worrying about failing the essay for my college course, I will make a list of the small steps I need to take and the research I need to carry out. I will tick off each step once I have completed it. This will help me to feel more optimistic about the task.'

4. Reflect on what you have learned from this task. How did you feel when you were using your strengths? What went well? Can you identify further opportunities to make the most of your top strengths? Did you need support to implement any of your ideas? If so, who or what could help you?

KEEP LEARNING

Aim: To identify opportunities to learn new things and develop your strengths in different ways.

How to do it: Learning new things has many benefits. Not only do we learn new skills and meet new people, but it is a chance to develop our strengths and improve our wellbeing. Through learning, we broaden our horizons, find new opportunities and increase our resilience.

1. Consider whether there was anything you did in the past that you enjoyed but no longer do (e.g. dancing, playing football, drawing, learning about history).

2. Make a list of things you would like to learn if you had the opportunity (e.g. gardening, baking, painting, sewing, yoga, biology).

3. Think about your current hobbies and interests, and consider whether there are any you would like to take further (e.g. if you enjoy looking after animals, you might consider getting a qualification in this that could lead to employment).

4. Now seek out opportunities to put one of these thoughts into action. Some possibilities could be:

   - Look at posters, noticeboards and newspapers in your local area to find out what is going on nearby.

   - Visit your local library to find books and resources on your topics of interest.

   - Find the websites of local colleges, universities and community centres to see what courses they offer under 'adult education'.

- Visit your local leisure centre to see the range of sporting opportunities on offer.

- Try out one of the free online learning courses on 'FutureLearn' (www.futurelearn.com), which include topics as diverse as politics, language, the environment, arts, literature, sciences and health and wellbeing.

- Consider a longer online course or distance learning leading to a qualification.

- Investigate local 'MeetUp' groups (www.meetup.com) in your area, or set one up yourself!

5. Once you have found some opportunities you would like to try out, discover more about these. You might need to send an email, make a phone call or visit to ask questions such as: What time does the activity take place? Where does it take place? Is there a cost? Do you need to bring anything? Is the activity suitable for beginners/improvers? If you have chosen something you want to work at independently at home, you will not need to complete this step.

6. Try out your new activity! You will often need to go along a few times before you get into the new routine and feel relaxed. Sometimes, you might need to try out several different options before you find a tutor and/or activity that suit you.

BEING A UNIQUE INDIVIDUAL

Aim: To develop a sense of self-identity to help you to seek out opportunities that are fulfilling to you as an individual.

How to do it: This activity can help you to identify what makes you 'you'. You can complete it in any way you like. You might like to write it down, draw a spider diagram, make a drawing or painting, create a collage, use the computer or any other way of expressing yourself.

1. Consider your top strengths. Write or draw these, along with examples of when you have used them.

2. What words would you use to describe yourself? Add these.

3. What words have others used to describe you? What compliments have they paid you? Add these to your diagram.

4. What are your likes, hobbies and interests? What is important to you? Add these too.

5. Add a list of your achievements. Achievements can be big or small – things that you have worked hard at, done well, or improved at.

6. You will see that you are a unique combination of traits, skills, attitudes and abilities. By recognising and celebrating these, you will better be able to channel your energy in a direction that is fulfilling to you as an individual. Take a look at your finished piece. Are there any patterns or themes? Continue to add to your piece as fresh ideas occur to you.

MY AUTISM AND ME

Aim: To identify how your autism affects you.

How to do it: Autism and Asperger syndrome are part of a spectrum of conditions; every individual is affected differently. You might have a good awareness of how your autism affects you, or you might only just be starting to learn about it. Consider your thoughts about the following questions.

1. What are the positives about your autism? Consider whether there is anything you feel you can do well and if there are any traits or skills that seem to come naturally to you. Have there been any times when your autistic traits have been an advantage?

2. Connecting and communicating with others is often a difference associated with the autism spectrum. How do you connect or communicate differently? Consider times when you are in groups, communicating one-to-one, and talking with familiar people or strangers. Are there situations you find easier than others?

3. Understanding the social world can be another difference. Are there situations you have found difficult to understand? How has your perspective differed from other people's?

4. Routines and structure can also be important for some individuals on the autism spectrum. Are there times when routine and structure are important to you? How does this affect you? Do you have any special interests?

5. Sensory sensitivities are another difference experienced by many individuals on the autism spectrum. Are you over- or under-sensitive to any sensory input (such as lights, noise, tastes, textures, smells)? What does this feel like for you?

6. Which aspects of your autism have you learned to cope with well? Are there things that used to be more difficult for you, but aren't now? If so, what strategies did you put into place and which skills did you use to overcome these?

7. What is your attitude towards your autism? Do you see it as a gift, an advantage, a disorder, a disability or a difference?

8. Add to these questions as you develop your understanding of your autism. Having a good understanding of how your autism affects you can help you become empowered.

You will be better able to identify what you need, which environments suit you and how others can help you.

Group activities

The following activities are designed for professionals to deliver with groups of individuals on the autism spectrum. Again, they are not prescriptive and should be adapted according to the ages, abilities and experiences of individuals in the group. Professionals might also wish to use some of the 'individual activities' with their group members.

WHAT ARE STRENGTHS?

Aim: To build up a strengths vocabulary and to help group members name strengths.

How to do it:

1. Use Appendix A: Strengths and Definitions. Ask the group members to work in pairs to match up the strengths with the definitions. This can be used as an ice-breaker activity to encourage communication and discussion within the group. Some groups might benefit from using smaller lists to make this task more manageable.

2. Go through the answers with the group. Emphasise that it does not matter if answers were wrong. The objective of this activity is to learn the new vocabulary. Use going through the answers as an opportunity to discuss what is meant by each word, perhaps giving examples of this strength in context and addressing any myths or misconceptions that group members have.

3. Choose a strengths word. Ask group members if they can identify any famous people who demonstrate that strength. They could also identify fictional characters,

or people they know in real life. The focus of this part of the session is on identifying how strengths can be used in different ways by different people. Encourage group members to give specific examples.

4. Now give group members time to consider what they think their own strengths are. Some might wish to think about this independently, while others might like to discuss it with a partner. Encourage group members to give specific examples of when they have used their strengths. If group members are struggling, ask them to consider a time when something has gone well or an activity that they very much enjoy doing – what strengths do they use in these situations? Perhaps other people have told them what their strengths are? If group members know each other well, they might be able to comment on each other's strengths.

5. Take feedback from those who wish to share the strengths they have identified. This activity leads on to the next one: 'Collect Your Strengths'.

COLLECT YOUR STRENGTHS

Aim: To support group members in identifying and recognising their strengths.

How to do it:

1. Ensure that group members are aware of what is meant by strengths. The previous activity might be a possible starting point. You could also give out the answer sheet in Appendix A as a reference sheet. A general discussion about strengths that group members have identified in famous people or in others might also be a starting point.

2. Ask group members to notice their strengths over the next week/fortnight (depending on how frequently the group meets). Ask each person to write down three things that have gone well, or that they think they did well each day. Then see if they can identify which strength they used in that situation. Example:

'I had a longer-than-usual wait in the dentist as she was running late. However, I remained calm and used the time to listen to my music. I demonstrated patience.'

3. At the next session, group members should have a list of strengths that they have demonstrated. Have they been using any strengths frequently? Were they surprised at how many strengths they have. Some group members who have difficulty in identifying strengths might need prompting and support to recognise these. Ask these individuals what has gone well for them during the week. From this, support them to identify the strengths they displayed in the event or situation.

SKILLS AND STRENGTHS SWAP

Aim: To provide an opportunity for group members to identify and use their strengths in order for other group members to benefit.

How to do it: This activity can be based around identified strengths and/or skills that group members possess. It is an opportunity for individuals to use one of their strengths or skills in a teaching or leading situation, and to learn new things from others. How this activity is delivered will depend very much on the number of participants and the strengths or skills chosen.

1. Ask group members to choose one of their top strengths or skills that they would like to teach to the rest of the group. Example:

   'I am very creative artistically and would like to teach the others how to draw animals.'

   'I am environmentally aware and would like to teach the others about recycling.'

   'I am very organised and want to share the system I have developed for organising myself and my household chores.'

2. Give group members time to prepare for the task. Some might need to bring examples or organise materials. Others might wish to create a computer presentation or poster. Some might benefit from making a planning sheet, or rehearsing what they will say.

3. Over the next sessions, facilitate these activities, giving each group member sufficient time to share their skill or strength. Encourage others to participate fully and ask any questions they might have while trying out the activities. This activity might also be an opportunity for group members to try out new activities in a non-threatening environment, before joining a club or group elsewhere.

WE'RE ALL UNIQUE

Aim: For group members to discuss their similarities and differences to support them in building up their self-identity.

How to do it: This activity could also be used as an ice-breaker for new groups to get to know each other, and can be an opportunity to develop communication and conversational skills.

1. Give each person a piece of paper and ask them to write down three hobbies or interests they have.

2. Ask group members to circulate around the room and try to find somebody who shares one of their hobbies or interests. Allow a few minutes for this task.

3. Ask the group for feedback. Did anybody find somebody with the same hobby or interest? Did anybody have a unique hobby or interest? If so, could they tell the group more about it?

4. Repeat steps 1–3, but this time the participants try to find mutual strengths instead of hobbies. Ask them for feedback in the same way.

5. This activity could also be done using different categories such as 'Places I like to go to', 'Words that describe me', 'Foods I like' or 'Animals I like'.

6. In the group discussion, reiterate how every person is unique, even though some of us might have some things in common.

AUTISM AND US

Aim: For group members to discuss how their autism affects them and to share successful coping strategies.

How to do it: As with other activities, this one might need to be adapted according to the individuals in the group. The activity might need to be facilitated carefully to ensure that an individual with particularly negative views does not influence others.

1. Begin by reiterating how autism is a spectrum and all individuals are affected in different ways. Explain how different people view autism differently – as a gift, disability or difference, for example. Some groups might

need additional input at this point, if they do not yet know much about the autism spectrum. Some useful videos are available from some of the organisations listed in the 'Further Reading and Resources' section of this book. You might also like to start by asking group members if they have any questions about the autism spectrum that they would like answered.

2. Split the whole group up into small groups of two or three people. Ask the groups to share anything that they find difficult because of their autism. After a few minutes, get some feedback from each group. Put the thoughts out to the whole group. Has anybody else experienced that difficulty and found an effective way of coping?

3. Now ask the groups to discuss what advantages or positives they think their autism brings to them. Again, ask for feedback and share it with the whole group.

4. Next ask the groups to discuss any coping strategies they have developed that help them to overcome any difficulties they face due to their autism. A coping strategy might be as simple as wearing ear defenders in a noisy place or going to the supermarket at a very quiet time. Again, ask the small groups to share their ideas with the whole group. Discuss how others in the group might try out or adapt similar coping strategies.

5. To finish, ask participants what advice they would give to their younger self. This often encourages individuals to reflect back on what has worked positively for them and on what they have learned as they have become older. Again, it can be an opportunity to share positive thoughts and coping strategies.

5

CULTIVATING POSITIVE EMOTIONS

This chapter considers how to cultivate positive emotions of happiness, hope, optimism, gratitude and appreciation. It is important to note that emotions cannot be neatly separated into 'positive' and 'negative' and nor should emotions be presented as such. There are no 'right' or 'wrong' emotions. Indeed, fear, anger, frustration, boredom, worry and many other less positive emotions can all be helpful. All emotions have evolved to serve a purpose. The aim is not to avoid or eliminate negative emotions but rather to be better able to recognise them and respond in more helpful ways. Take an individual who is worried about an upcoming driving test, for example. This worry could be positive; it may encourage the person to focus on practise and revision for the theoretical component, therefore approaching the test with increased confidence and knowledge. If the person was not worried, they might approach the test without doing so much preparation, and thereby increase the likelihood of failure. A little bit of worry can, in such a case, be motivating. If, however, the worry became overwhelming, the individual might spend so much time caught up in worrying thoughts, that they might be unable to focus on revising and might approach the test in such a state of worry that they are unable to think clearly and safely. It is not emotions themselves that can be negative, but more our response to them.

That said, there are generally some emotions that are usually considered more 'positive', or pleasant, to experience. These include excitement, joy, interest, satisfaction, contentment, fulfilment, gratitude, calm, zest, pleasure, hope, faith, humour and trust, to name just a few. Cultivating these emotions can bring many benefits and increase satisfaction with life. Barbara Fredrickson's 'broaden and build' theory (2002) shows how experiencing positive emotions leads to an upwards spiral of more positive emotions, opportunities for personal growth, and further positive emotions. In contrast, negative emotions narrow our focus, thoughts and behaviours. There is also evidence that experiencing positive emotions can act as a 'reset button' (Fredrickson *et al.* 2000), taking us back closer to our original state of being, and helping to reduce the impact of the more 'negative' emotion. 'Reset buttons' could include doing something physical (e.g. exercise, walking, gardening), making a connection with somebody or something you care for (e.g. people, pets, charity work), doing something to make your body feel calmer (e.g. having a bath, massage, relaxation, meditation), doing an activity that takes your mind off things (e.g. cooking, cleaning, singing, reading, crosswords), or thinking about things differently (e.g. accepting the situation, reframing the situation, journalling, counting blessings) (LeBon 2014).

HAPPINESS, JOY AND INSPIRATION

The concept of personal happiness has gained increased attention in the past decades. Now that the majority of people in economically developed countries have their basic needs met (i.e. food, water, medical supplies, housing, education), their attention has shifted beyond what is needed for survival, and towards looking at what can improve their happiness and sense of wellbeing.

'Happy' is a word we use often but one that is notoriously difficult to define. What makes one person happy may make another person very unhappy. Happiness may mean different things to different people at different times. It can mean having fun, being yourself, loving others, doing something meaningful, enjoying hobbies, learning new skills, feeling safe and valued, accepting and appreciating what you have, making new discoveries, finding the joy in everyday moments, working towards goals, and feeling part of something bigger. Researchers have found that the most commonly cited answers to the 'What makes you happy?' question are relationships, health, contentment, security, personal achievements and concerns for others (Boniwell and Ryan 2012).

Historically, the concept of 'happiness' has been much debated. The Greek philosopher Aristotle believed that simply 'feeling good' is not enough for happiness; true happiness only happens when individuals feel they are living a good life on a wider scale. He argued that happiness depends on acquiring a moral character when one displays the virtues of courage, generosity, justice, friendship and citizenship in one's life. For Aristotle, happiness was, therefore, more a question of behaviour and habit; a person who cultivates such behaviours and habits is able to bear misfortunes with balance and perspective, and thus can never be said to be truly unhappy (Burton 2013).

Modern research also shows that while pursuing pleasurable activities may increase short-term happiness, pursuing personal growth and greater meaning is more likely to increase longer-term happiness. The positive psychology movement also considers these various 'layers' of happiness. Martin Seligman (2002), one of the leading experts in the positive psychology movement, recognises three aspects of happiness: the pleasant life (the pursuit of positive emotions), the good life (using one's strengths, experiencing flow), and the meaningful life (using one's strengths in the service of something greater than oneself). In this chapter, we explore strategies for increasing positive experiences and short-term happiness, as well as considering how 'happiness' might be realised in the longer term.

KEY TERMS

Subjective wellbeing: A term often used in the research literature instead of 'happiness'. Using this term helps to overcome some of the vagueness and ambiguity associated with the word 'happiness'. Happiness can mean different things to different people and can refer to an ongoing state of wellbeing, or a one-off pleasurable activity. Measuring 'happiness' often relies on using self-evaluations, hence the term 'subjective'.

Flourishing: In his 2011 book, *Flourish*, Martin Seligman explains how he now considers the term 'happiness' to be overused and almost meaningless. He prefers to use the term 'flourishing' to encompass the value more accurately; flourishing comes from gaining meaning and purpose in our life, experiencing personal growth and feeling part of something bigger than ourselves.

The benefits of happiness and flourishing

It may seem obvious that happiness is a good thing, so something that we should strive for. But what does the research tell us?

- A body of research by Barbara Fredrickson (2009) shows that happier students learn and perform better in the classroom than unhappier students. Happier students tend to be more creative, focused, persistent and energetic.

- Happy people tend to work harder and are more likely to succeed. Happier children have even been found to earn higher salaries when they are adults (Judge and Hurst 2007).

- Happy people have better friendships and relationships. They are also more likely to be trusting of others and to help others (Boniwell and Ryan 2012).

- Happy people tend to be more creative and show divergent thinking. They are also more likely to persist longer at less enjoyable tasks, and are more systematic and attentive (Lyubomirsky, King and Diener 2005).

- Happiness has also been linked with living a longer life (Danner, Snowdon and Friedsen 2001).

Flow

'Flow' is a term coined by positive psychologist Mikhail Csikszentmihalyi and is considered to be another key element of human flourishing. Being immersed in 'flow' has been likened to being effortlessly pulled forward like the flow of a river, hence the name. Athletes often refer to 'being in the zone'; when they talk about this they are referring to being in 'flow'. You do not have to be a world-class athlete to experience it – we can all experience flow whatever our age, background, or activity we are engaged in.

Flow experiences share some important characteristics (Csikszentmihalyi 1992):

- **Complete concentration on the task in hand at the present moment:** The mind is not wandering or thinking about the past or future.

- **Clear goals and immediate feedback:** You know what it is you need to focus on and are getting immediate feedback on your progress (e.g. in a sport, you know if you are winning or losing).

- **Feeling 'at one' with the activity:** Your actions and awareness become merged so that you do not feel separate from the task. A musician, for example, may become the music that he plays, with the involvement feeling almost effortless.

- **Loss of self-consciousness:** You may lose awareness of yourself and experience feelings of calm and serenity.

- **A sense of control over what you are doing:** You feel that you know what to do next and do not worry about failure.

- **Time passing in different ways:** Time seems to 'fly by' without you realising.

- **Intrinsic motivation:** You feel that what you are doing is rewarding for its own sake, with other end goals being less important.

The sense of flow happens under specific circumstances – the activity needs to be well matched to our level of skill. If the challenge is too difficult for our skill level, then we are less likely to experience flow as we will find the task too hard and can feel anxious about this. If the challenge is too easy for our skill level, then there is a good chance we will become bored. Flow usually occurs when we are engaged in something that challenges us, but at a level that is just possible for us to meet. Therefore, watching TV is not usually considered to be an activity that generates flow, due to its passivity. However, blind people often quote television-watching as a flow activity (Boniwell 2008) as it is more challenging for them – they have to build mental images of what is going on in the absence of being able to see the screen.

Flow is considered beneficial because of its lasting effects – when we are in 'flow' we do not notice it, but afterwards we will feel happier, fulfilled and have a sense of achievement. However, flow is not necessarily always a good thing as there are also some potential pitfalls to activities that might create a sense of 'flow':

- Some 'flow' activities may be morally concerning (e.g. activities that cause harm to oneself, other people or property).

- Some 'flow' activities can become addictive (e.g. computer games, gambling) – this can have a negative impact on the individual's life, and can make life without the addiction feel boring and meaningless.

Many individuals on the autism spectrum have a 'special interest', an interest that they are passionate and intense about. The 'special interest' often plays a large part in their life; it may dominate their time, thoughts and conversation. A 'special' interest goes much further than a regular hobby or interest. There can often be an emphasis on collecting, cataloguing and categorising. There may be repetitive actions and behaviours, set routines around the special interest, or a huge factual knowledge of related statistics. Special interests can range from quantum physics to collecting bottle tops. Whatever the interest, it can be an opportunity for individuals to reduce stress, increase feelings of wellbeing and to experience flow. Research suggests that some of the repetitive activities that accompany special interests can help to achieve a 'flow' state of mind (McDonell and Milton 2014).

However, some hobbies and interests can be more addictive. Computer games, for example, are actually designed to optimise flow and keep people playing. This can then have a negative impact on other areas of life – work may not get done, players might get insufficient sleep or they might neglect other important tasks (e.g. washing), which can then lead to lower mood and frustration.

Happiness and autism

Individuals on the autism spectrum experience the same range of positive emotions as any other person, although there may sometimes be some differences in how these are expressed or interpreted. Evidence also indicates that individuals on the autism spectrum may be more likely than their neurotypical counterparts to experience feelings of unhappiness, depression and worry (Hudson, Hall and Harkness 2018; Van Heijst and Guerts 2014). The exact reasons will differ from individual to individual, but some possible reasons for them being 'less happy' could include:

- Experiencing feelings of isolation or loneliness due to difficulties making and maintaining friendships and relationships.

- Feeling 'different' or 'odd' and not fitting in with others.

- Having low self-esteem and self-worth as a result of previous negative experiences.

- Feeling misunderstood by others.

- Misunderstanding others' intentions.

- Difficulties in communicating their needs and perspectives clearly and coherently.

- Difficulties in understanding and expressing their own emotions and the emotions of others.

- Having to try very hard at things that seem to come so easily to others.

- Being told by others that they are 'wrong', that they need to try harder, or that their feelings and perspectives are not as valid as other people's.

- A history of negative experiences of education and employment, meaning they feel they are not working to their possible potential.

- Being more vulnerable to bullying, discrimination or perceived bullying.

- Anxiety when in public places, or the workplace, because of sensory overload.

- Finding socialising difficult or exhausting.

- Difficulties forming relationships with family members.

- General anxiety about everyday events, particularly if there are changes to routines or inconsistent rules.

- Not having their difficulties or differences recognised by others.

- Not understanding why they are 'different' to others, particularly if they have not yet received a diagnosis, or have not received appropriate support post-diagnosis.

- Not seeing their values and perspectives reflected back in mainstream culture and the media.

- Lacking a solid sense of self-identity.

- Lacking confidence in their own perspectives and opinions.

Research has also indicated that negative comparisons and inequality increase unhappiness (Ni 2014). Internal comparisons can also affect our levels of happiness. If the life we are living is close to our ideal or how we think we 'should' live, then we are likely to be happier than if there is a substantial discrepancy between our present conditions and our 'ideal' vision (Boniwell 2008). Our 'ideal' is likely to be influenced by the media, our family, culture and the society in which we are brought up. Relating this to autism, it is easy to see why some autistic individuals may be less happy than others. The 'ideal' image we are often bombarded with through mass media includes having lots of friends, having a great social life, following a certain lifestyle, adhering to a certain physical image and having material success. For less typical individuals, it can be difficult to feel happy in their own skin if they are constantly being told they should be different.

It is important for individuals on the autism spectrum to identify what makes them happy as an individual, not what they think should make them happy. What makes an autistic person happy may not be what makes a non-autistic person happy. It is important to avoid forcing autistic people into a neurotypical concept of happiness (Vermeulen 2016). Equally, what makes one autistic person happy may not be what makes another autistic person happy. Happiness is unique to individuals, therefore the strategies that follow later in this chapter are not prescriptive but encourage individuals to explore what works for them.

Paradoxically, it is also important not to focus too much on 'being happy' as an outcome. Evidence suggests that the more that people worry about being happy, the less happy they become (Blyth 2013).

HOPE AND OPTIMISM

Being hopeful and optimistic can also improve wellbeing. Being hopeful reflects a positive expectation about something happening in the future. This helps people to stay healthy, to improve performance and to cope with difficulties in life. It is thought that being hopeful:

- Helps to reduce self-critical thoughts

- Increases focus on the positives

- Enables people to create a mental plan

- Increases focus and motivation

- Helps us to achieve goals

- Contributes to our feelings of happiness and wellbeing

Hopeful adults focus on success rather than failure, experience fewer negative feelings when encountering obstacles, and are more able to break down large, vague tasks into small, manageable problems (Snyder 2000).

KEY TERMS

Optimists: Optimists have a sense of confidence about the future. They generally expect outcomes to be positive.

Pessimists: Pessimists generally expect outcomes to be negative. They have a sense of doubt and hesitancy.

Positive psychology research has found many advantages to optimistic thinking (Boniwell 2008). Optimists tend to be able to deal with difficulties more positively, adapt better to negative events and learn lessons from negatives. They are also less likely to give up, engage more in health-promoting behaviours and seem more productive in the workplace.

Being hopeful is not just about wishful thinking and blithely ignoring any negatives. It is about looking at things positively yet realistically. It involves acknowledging any possible setbacks or difficulties, and planning how to deal with these in a positive way. Optimistic thinking alone is associated with underestimating risks (Peterson and Park 2003), and further research has shown that extreme optimism can lead to over-confidence (Ifcher and Zarghamee 2011).

In general, humans have a 'negativity bias' – a tendency to notice the more negative things, people and events. We are all more likely to remember the one negative comment we received, rather than the ten positive ones, or remember the bad day of our holiday rather than the six positive days! This negativity bias developed as an evolutionary adaptation for our species – noticing dangers, fear and anger has been necessary in the past for the survival of the human race.

Neuroscientists are also discovering that our brain can be shaped by what we pay attention to. So, for example, if we keep resting our mind on good events and conditions, then over time different neural pathways will be strengthened than if our mind keeps resting on self-criticism, worries and stress; in the latter case our brain would be shaped into greater reactivity and vulnerability towards anxiety and depression, rather than into a more optimistic outlook (Hanson 2013).

Hope, optimism and autism

Some evidence suggests that individuals on the autism spectrum may be more susceptible to a negativity bias when it comes to forming beliefs about future outcomes (Kuzmanovic, Rigoux and Vogeley 2016). Some specific challenges for individuals on the autism spectrum in having an optimistic outlook might include:

- **Literal thinking:** A literal interpretation of language and events can lead to possible misunderstandings and corresponding negative expectations about future events. Words such as 'can't' or 'don't' might be interpreted in their most literal sense.

- **Difficulties with social interaction:** If individuals frequently find it difficult to socialise with others or have a history of previous misunderstandings, they might feel less confident about future situations.

- **Environmental/sensory sensitivities:** These can increase anxiety and levels of frustration in individuals on the autism spectrum, making it harder to concentrate and to think hopefully.

- **Low self-esteem:** This can affect levels of confidence and belief about the future.

- **Fear of failure:** Some individuals on the autism spectrum may have perfectionist tendencies. In combination with low self-esteem and over-generalising (e.g. 'I have failed my driving test, so I'm a failure in all aspects of life') this can lead to restricting beliefs and behaviours about the future.

- **Executive functioning:** Executive functioning involves the skills needed in planning, sequencing, organising, prioritising, remembering and carrying out tasks. This can be an area of difficulty for some individuals on the autism spectrum (Attwood 2007) and can affect how future goals are approached.

- **Need for sameness and routine:** This can mean some individuals on the autism spectrum may not look forward to future events – the anxiety about change can outweigh any excitement they might feel.

- **Theory of Mind and alexithymia:** It can be difficult for individuals on the autism spectrum to understand and predict other people's (and their own) thoughts, feelings and perspectives. Again, this might increase the likelihood of misunderstandings or anxiety. It might also be difficult for some individuals to predict how they will feel in future situations.

As always, not all of these points will affect every individual on the autism spectrum, and every individual will be affected differently. These are just some possible challenges that some might face; many individuals on the autism spectrum can, and do, develop positive and optimistic attitudes.

KEY TERMS

Theory of Mind: The ability to understand that other people have different perspectives, thoughts and beliefs to one's own.

Alexithymia: The difficulty in recognising and describing emotions and feelings in oneself.

GRATITUDE AND APPRECIATION

Studies have shown that being grateful is strongly associated with happiness, wellbeing and life satisfaction (Emmons 2007; Lyubomirsky 2007). Gratitude is about not taking life for granted and works on different levels – being grateful to people, being grateful for opportunities, being grateful for experiences and being grateful for the life force around us and within us.

Gratitude interventions (e.g. counting blessings, being thankful and recording what went well) have been investigated with powerful results. Such interventions have been shown to increase happiness and reduce depressive symptoms for up to six months (Seligman *et al.* 2005). Recognising feelings of gratitude can help us to focus on the good things in our life and therefore helps to increase our wellbeing and level of life-satisfaction.

Kindness and gratitude

Kindness is about doing nice things for other people, not for our own personal benefit but for the positive impact on the other person. Research shows that doing kind acts for others makes people happier. There can be a number of reasons for this – doing kind acts for others can help us to connect with them and can also help us to feel more confident and optimistic about our ability to make a difference. Kind acts also help us to feel more positive about other people and the community we live in (Lyubormirsky, Sheldon and Schkade 2005). Kindness has been shown to have a benefit for both the 'giver' and the 'receiver'.

There are many books, projects and websites now dedicated to 'random acts of kindness' and, while these generally advocate doing kind deeds for others, the focus should always be on the impact on the other person, and not about 'doing kind acts' for more self-centred reasons of increasing our own happiness levels.

Gratitude and autism

Individuals on the autism spectrum have the same capacity to experience and recognise gratitude as any other individual. What is important, however, is that 'neurotypical' beliefs and opinions are not forced onto the autistic individual. Some of the things that a neurotypical individual might feel grateful for (e.g. being able to spend the day socialising with friends) might actually increase anxiety and feelings of difference in the individual on the autism spectrum. It might be that the individual on the autism spectrum can identify certain aspects of the day that they feel grateful for (e.g. 'I have good friends who invited me out'), but it is important they do not feel 'forced' to feel grateful for something that invoked uncomfortable feelings for them or increased their anxiety levels. This can simply create additional confusion (e.g. 'I've been told I *should* be grateful that I have such sociable housemates, but really I just want to read my book in peace. What's wrong with me?').

Some individuals on the autism spectrum have differences in how they interpret other people's thoughts and intentions (difficulties with 'Theory of Mind'). Equally, many neurotypical people also have difficulty in interpreting the thoughts and perspectives of autistic people. It is usually a two-way problem! This can sometimes lead to difficulties with experiencing gratitude from both sides; for example, an intended act of kindness might be interpreted as having the opposite effect. Take this instance:

Suranne, an individual on the autism spectrum, sees that a friend, Ella, is upset. She leaves Ella alone, as this is what she would like others to do with her – when she is upset, the last thing that she feels like doing is having to cope with communicating with other people. She also feels uncomfortable when people hug her and this increases her anxiety. However, Ella interprets Suranne leaving her alone as her friend not being supportive and not caring about her being upset.

POSITIVE EMOTIONS: PUTTING IT INTO PRACTICE
Individual activities

The following activities are designed for individuals on the autism spectrum to work through independently. There is no 'right way' to complete these activities. You might like to write, draw, type, make a collage or simply think about your answers. Professionals working on a one-to-one basis with individuals on the autism spectrum might also like to guide their clients through some of these. Many activities are designed to be used as a starting point for further discussion and deeper exploration.

WHAT MAKES YOU HAPPY?

Aim: To identify what brings you happiness, joy and inspiration.

How to do it:

1. Decide how you would like to complete this activity. You might want to make a list, draw a spider diagram, make a collage or complete it in any other way.

2. Write or draw all of the things that make you happy. You might like to consider:

   • Hobbies or interests that you enjoy doing

   • Places you enjoy visiting

   • People you enjoy spending time with

   • Things that make you smile and laugh

- Times you have felt alive, excited or curious

- Small things that bring joy to your day

- Times you feel loved and valued

- Things you've done in the past that you enjoyed

- Times you feel totally engaged with an activity you are doing

3. You might need to add to this over time, as you recall things that make you happy. Once complete, take a look at your list. Do you make time every week for the things that make you happy? If not, are there things that you could do more frequently or build into your daily routine?

'I'LL BE HAPPY NOW'

Aim: To evaluate any limiting beliefs you have about what it means to be happy.

How to do it: Many of us have thoughts such as 'I'll be happy when I...have more money/a better job/a partner/a bigger house'. These sorts of thoughts tend to make us less happy as we are finding excuses to delay being happy. We are criticising the present and comparing it with an ideal future. In reality, things such as new possessions, a new job or a larger salary tend only to bring short-term happiness. In the meantime we are not allowing ourselves to be happy.

1. Consider whether you have any beliefs that are stopping you being happy in the present. Are you 'waiting' to be happy? Write down what your beliefs are. Examples:

'I'll be happy if I have a different job.'

'I'll be happier when I'm earning more money.'

'I'd be happier if I wasn't on the autism spectrum.'

2. Evaluate where these beliefs come from. Many of our beliefs arise simply because of what we have been exposed to in the media or they are an accumulation of the beliefs all around us. Challenge your beliefs. Example:

'I'd be happier if I wasn't on the autism spectrum.'

Thought challenge: 'I know this isn't really true as I know plenty of people who are not on the autism spectrum who are unhappy. I also know people on the autism spectrum who are happy!'

3. Consider all the things that you are happy with and that are going well in your life. Choose to be happy now instead of postponing your happiness. Examples:

'I'd be happy if I had a different job.'

'I don't really like my current job but that doesn't mean I can't be happy with the other aspects of my life. There are also some elements of my job I can be happy with, and I can begin to look for a new job too.'

WHY PUT OFF...?

Aim: To identify whether there is anything you are putting off rather than doing that would make you happier.

How to do it:

1. Many of us have things that we think would make us happier (e.g. having a hobby, joining a group, getting a new job, having a pet, doing more exercise). It can be easy to delay doing these things by saying things like, 'I'll do it when I have more time', 'I'll do it when I feel more confident about it', 'I'll do it when I'm feeling more motivated'. Identify if there is anything you are putting off and think about the reasons you are giving yourself for not doing these things.

2. The reality is that we only become more confident about doing new things by actually doing them. If we keep waiting until we feel more confident, that day is likely never to come. Make a plan to do one of the things you keep putting off. Set yourself small targets to meet and write down a plan of the steps you need to take.

REFRAMING

Aim: To reframe less helpful experiences to support happiness and positivity.

How to do it: Sometimes we get stuck in a pattern of thought, focusing perhaps only on the negatives or one aspect of the situation. Use this activity to help you see situations or experiences from a different angle.

1. Identify a negative thought you have or a situation or circumstance that you feel unhappy about. Example:

   'I hate my job.'

2. Next, try reframing this thought to highlight what it indicates. Example:

   'Knowing I'm unhappy in my office work shows me that I'd be better suited to a job in which I can use my practical skills and my love of nature.'

3. Thinking about a situation differently might help you to identify positive steps you can take to improve the situation. Example:

   'I could start looking for jobs that are based outdoors. I could volunteer at a weekend in the forest to gain some new skills.'

CATCHING UNHOPEFUL SELF-TALK

Aim: To change unhopeful self-talk to more positive self-talk.

How to do it:

1. Consider whether there are any situations that you feel less hopeful about, or any recurring unhopeful thoughts you experience. Example:

    'I won't enjoy going to my friend's wedding at the weekend as I hate events like that.'

2. Consider how you could change this thought to a more hopeful statement. Example:

    'I don't usually enjoy going to big social events but I'm grateful that my friend invited me to his wedding. I'll enjoy watching him get married and I don't have to stay long at the party afterwards.'

3. Try using this technique to move to a more hopeful state of mind about future events. It can also help you to identify what you can put into place to help you cope more effectively in upcoming situations.

BEST- AND WORST-CASE SCENARIOS

Aim: To use 'realistic optimism' as a tool to plan for future events and to support more hopeful thoughts and attitudes.

How to do it:

1. We all have situations that we feel nervous or worried about. This might mean that we experience anxiety leading up to the event or that we try to avoid the event. Consider whether there is anything you are worried about.

2. Next consider what the best possible outcome of this situation could be. Then consider the worst-case scenario. Example:

   Situation: 'I've been invited to go away for the weekend with a group of friends, but it is causing me anxiety.'

   Best-case scenario: 'I have an enjoyable weekend with friends. I chat to them and enjoy their company. I feel relaxed and confident. We laugh a lot and have fun. I see some new places and enjoy looking around a new city.'

   Worst-case scenario: 'I am worried for weeks in advance. I am nervous all weekend and worried we might do something I don't enjoy. I get exhausted having to socialise and so I become quiet and withdrawn. I wish I hadn't gone and I spend the weekend wishing I was at home. My friends wonder why I am miserable and tell me I am ruining the weekend.'

3. In reality, most situations will usually fall somewhere between the two extremes. However, considering the worst that could happen can help us to plan for these eventualities. Example:

   'I could ask my friends in advance what we might be doing over the weekend. I will thank them for inviting me and I will tell them that sometimes I need some more time to myself. If I feel I am becoming exhausted, I could go back to the hotel for a rest or go for a walk by myself. I will make sure my friends know I enjoy their company but at times I just need some time away from too much sensory stimulation. That way, I'll be more energised when I am with them.'

4. See if this technique can help you plan for any upcoming situations you are worried about.

OPTIMISTIC PLANNING

Aim: To plan realistically yet optimistically.

How to do it: It can be easy to become overwhelmed by upcoming events. We might begin to panic about them, or be unsure where to start and what to do. Instead of being productive, we might find ourselves worrying about the event or attempting to avoid it. Try using these prompts to break down the problem into smaller steps.

1. What is the event or situation? Define it as specifically as possible and state the deadline for it.

2. Break the bigger problem down into the smaller steps that you will need to take along the way.

3. List the strengths and skills you bring to this problem. What are your strengths? What skills do you have? When have you overcome similar issues in the past?

4. What questions do you have or what do you need to find out to make progress in this situation? Write down specific questions. Where could you find the answers – books, websites, friends, family, colleagues, online forums, a mentor, a local service or organisation?

5. Who do you have around you who could help you with this situation? Think about friends, family members, colleagues, mentors, support groups, social workers. Be specific about the support you need.

6. Work through your plan. Celebrate the small successes along the way and don't be afraid to change your plan if you realise there are more effective ways of doing things once you start.

KEEPING A GRATITUDE DIARY

Aim: To identify and appreciate what is going well in your life.

How to do it: It can be easy to focus on the negatives or things that have not gone so well for us – humans have an in-built 'negativity bias'. The keeping of a gratitude journal has been shown to increase feelings of positivity.

1. Use a notepad, your phone, computer or other method of recording. At the end of each day, write down three things that you are grateful for, or that have gone well. These could include: people in your life, pets in your life, the natural environment, things you have seen or heard, events you attended, situations you enjoyed, things you did well, opportunities you have had, activities that you enjoyed, freedoms you have, nice moments during your day, or things that made you laugh or smile.

2. Try to identify different things each day, rather than the same things. Think back over your day – the things you note down do not have to be big things.

3. Keep up the activity for a week, a month or longer. At the end of each week, read back over your notes and remember all of the nice moments and things you are grateful for.

Group activities

The following activities are designed for professionals to deliver with groups of individuals on the autism spectrum. Again, they are not prescriptive and should be adapted according to the ages, abilities and experiences of individuals in the group. Professionals might also wish to use some of the 'individual activities' with their clients.

A HAPPINESS SURVEY

Aim: To recognise the different things that make different people happy.

How to do it: Again, this activity is designed to have the secondary objective of facilitating communication and conversational skills. Depending on the group and setting, you might decide to begin this activity with a discussion or recapping of how to initiate, maintain and end conversations.

1. Group members might prefer to work independently or in pairs. Ask them to design a 'survey' to answer the question 'What makes you happy?' They could try to generate around ten possible answers for respondents to choose from. Reiterate that all of these surveys will be different and group members can interpret the question how they wish. Example:

   What makes you happy?

   Choose up to three answers:

   Spending time with friends

   Spending time with family

   Being with my pets

   Visiting the countryside

   Being in nature

   Doing my hobby

   Playing sport

   Reading

   Learning new things

   Relaxing

2. Once the surveys have been designed, facilitate the session so that group members can circulate amongst others and ask them to give their answers. Remind participants that there are no right or wrong answers and that everybody will have their own opinions.

3. To finish the session, ask if any group members would like to give feedback on their results. Discuss the fact that we all have different things that make us happy and that what makes one person happy might not make another person happy. This is part of the diversity of being human. Some group members might also like to share the specific things that make them happy or discuss how they could do more of the things that make them happy.

HAPPINESS DEBATE

Aim: To spark discussion and dispel some myths surrounding happiness.

How to do it: Encourage participants to play 'devil's advocate' and identify counter-arguments, even if that is not what they believe themselves, to spark discussion. You might be able to gain an insight into what participants believe will make them happy and some of the limiting beliefs they hold. This activity can also be used to support communication skills such as being assertive, negotiation and compromise.

1. Display the happiness statements below, one at a time. You might choose to display them on a board, screen or large piece of paper. Alternatively, they can simply be read aloud. You might wish to choose the statements most relevant to your group, or add some of your own. Example:

   'Money makes people happy.'

   'Good-looking people are happier.'

'Living in a big house makes you happy.'

'Having a partner makes you happy.'

'Having lots of possessions makes you happy.'

'People are either born happy or born unhappy.'

'People can become happier throughout their life.'

'Other people can make you unhappy.'

'If a lot of bad things happen to you, you will be unhappy.'

2. After displaying each statement and giving group members time to consider it, ask them to decide whether they agree or disagree. Ask those who agree to move to one side of the room, and those who disagree to move to the other.

3. Ask if anybody would like to share their thoughts. Remind group members that there are no right or wrong answers; these statements are merely to spark discussion. Ask those with opposing views to share their reasoning. The group does not have to come to a final agreement but can agree to differ.

OPTIMIST VERSUS PESSIMIST

Aim: To understand the difference between optimism and pessimism.

How to do it: This activity can be delivered by splitting the main group into two (one group to take on the role of 'optimists' and the other of 'pessimists'), or by asking the group to work in pairs, with one person taking on the role of 'optimist' and the other of 'pessimist'.

1. Give out one set of the cards provided in Appendix E to each pair. If delivering this activity in a whole group situation, simply read the cards aloud, one at a time.

2. Ask the designated 'optimists' to think of an optimistic response to that situation, and the designated 'pessimists' to consider a pessimistic response. (There are no 'right' or 'wrong' answers as such, and various suggestions might be made. The main aim is to support an understanding of 'optimism' and 'pessimism'.)

3. You might like to switch the groups halfway through to give all participants the opportunity to practise both optimistic and pessimistic thinking. Example:

   Situation card (from Appendix E): You have made some new friends at a sports club you go to and wonder if they would like to go for coffee and cake one day after training.

   Possible optimistic thought: 'I can make the suggestion. Some might be busy or not able to make it, but others might like to come.'

   Possible pessimistic thought: 'Nobody will want to socialise with me and they will all say "no". I won't bother asking them.'

4. You might like to ask participants if they feel they have a tendency for one way of thinking. Can anybody share examples?

5. To develop this activity, discuss the possible consequences of both extremes. Choose some of the situations and discuss what an extreme pessimistic response might lead to, and then an extreme optimistic response. Explain to the group that being too pessimistic might lead to you avoiding situations and fearing the worst, while being too

optimistic might mean that you fail to prepare adequately for some situations. A better response is that of 'realistic optimism', being optimistic but planning realistically.

FROM UNHOPEFUL TO HOPEFUL

Aim: To recognise the difference between hopeful and unhopeful statements.

How to do it:

1. Depending on the group, this activity can also be delivered to the whole group, or by dividing the group into pairs. Give out the 'unhopeful statements' in Appendix F to each pair, or read/display them to the whole group.

2. Ask if each pair can try to change each of these statements to a more 'hopeful' statement. Example:

   Unhopeful statement: 'I'll never be able to drive a car.'

   More hopeful statement: 'I can't drive a car yet, but with practice I'm sure I can get better.'

3. Take feedback. Once again, there are multiple 'right' answers for each statement. Explain to the group that we might hear ourselves talk or think in this unhopeful manner, which can lead to us dwelling on negatives. Invite group members to share any examples of their own unhopeful thinking. Encourage them to rephrase their own thoughts to more hopeful alternatives.

THE BEST AND THE WORST OF IT

Aim: To understand that most situations are not going to be as bad as we fear.

How to do it:

1. Consider a situation that your group is likely to worry about or avoid due to anxiety (e.g. work-related, social-related, dealing with services, travel, accessing the community).

2. Describe the situation. Ask one half of the group to consider what could be the best possible outcome. Ask the other half to consider the worst-case scenario. Example:

   Situation: I've been invited to give a presentation about autism at a local college.

   Best-case scenario: I speak clearly and confidently. The students are interested and ask questions at the end that I can answer. I have a clear presentation that everybody can read. I remember everything I wanted to say and I speak loudly enough. I feel confident and enjoy myself. I get good feedback and am asked to speak again.

   Worst-case scenario: I am shaking with nerves and forget everything I want to say. My voice is quiet and squeaky. Nobody can hear me and they all look bored. My presentation won't display on the screen. Nobody asks any questions and the feedback is awful.

3. Take feedback from the groups. Explain how, in reality, something between these two extremes is most likely to happen. However, by considering the worst-case scenario, we can plan for the situation and increase our preparedness. In the example above, we might make notes to refer to, take a bottle of water with us, rehearse in advance and arrive early to set up the technology. In the situation you have used, consider what preparations individuals could make to help them feel more prepared and increase the likelihood of more positive outcomes.

THREE GOOD THINGS

Aim: To identify things that are going well and to encourage feelings of gratitude and appreciation.

How to do it:

1. This activity might be used at the beginning of a session, or at the end, depending on the setting and circumstances. Ask each group member to identify three things that have gone well or that they are grateful for. This might be three things that have happened in the past week since you last met as a group or, if delivering this activity at the end of a session, three good things that have happened during the day.

2. Remind group members that these 'good things' could include nice things others have said or done, people or animals they have had contact with, things they have noticed in their natural environment, things that have made them laugh or smile, opportunities they have had, activities they have enjoyed.

3. Ask each group member to share one of their good things. If time permits, you might ask group members to share two or three. This can be an opportunity for discussion and to reflect on the positive things in each of the participants' lives. Encourage group members to identify different things rather than the same things each week. Some participants might need support to identify things that have gone well – help these individuals to begin to notice small things around them – maybe they watched a butterfly while they were waiting for the bus or enjoyed the warmth of the sun when they were walking home.

6

POSITIVE COPING

We have already looked at how to cultivate more positive emotions and experiences. However, there are always going to be times in life that are more difficult. Experiencing emotions such as sadness, grief, disappointment, fear, anger, worry and frustration is a natural and expected part of being human. This chapter does not suggest we avoid or eliminate these emotions but that we learn how to cope with them effectively and positively, rather than letting them become overwhelming.

RESILIENCE
What is resilience?

Resilience is the ability to 'bounce back' from adversity. We are all likely to encounter times of stress, disappointment, loss, failure or trauma. People who are resilient are able to learn from these times and move on effectively. People who are less resilient find these times harder – it might take them longer to overcome negative experiences and they might let one negative experience influence all aspects of their life.

Why is resilience important?

Resilient individuals are able to restore positive mental and emotional health following a challenging or adverse situation. Resilient individuals do not become overwhelmed by small setbacks and are able to cope with the ups and downs of everyday life. Being resilient has a positive impact on emotional wellbeing.

How do we become resilient?

Resilience has now been shown to be learnable and teachable (Rae 2016). It is not something that we are born with. Both adults and children can learn strategies that will help them to become more resilient and learn from prior experiences. Neuroscientists believe that repeated mental activities leave enduring neural imprints on our brain. For example, if you routinely practise relaxation, this will increase the activity of the genes that calm down stress reactions, making you more resilient. Scientists call this 'experience-dependent-neuroplasticity' (Hanson 2013).

Each individual can use different strengths, talents and tools to increase their resilience. Some examples of individual qualities that can facilitate resilience include:

- Relationships with others

- Humour

- Inner direction/self-motivation

- Independence

- Optimism

- Flexibility/adaptability

- Love of learning

- Spirituality

- Self-acceptance

- Communication skills

Taking care of wellbeing through sleep, exercise and healthy eating can also increase resilience (it is much harder to cope with negativity when hungry and tired!), and improving emotional literacy can also be beneficial.

Resilience and autism

Individuals on the autism spectrum can learn to improve their level of resilience, just as any other individual can. Some specific challenges for some individuals on the autism spectrum might include:

- Experiencing low self-esteem

- Having a lack of confidence in their own ability, especially if they have received a lot of support in the past, have not been given the opportunity to cope independently, or have received negative reactions from others

- Fixed or rigid thinking

- Differences in how they communicate and interact with others

- Having a literal interpretation of language and situations

- Difficulties in recognising and understanding feelings and emotions, both in themselves (alexithymia) and in others

GROWTH MINDSET OR FIXED MINDSET

Our mindset affects our overall sense of wellbeing and influences how we approach challenges and opportunities. The mindset that we approach life with will determine whether we see problems or challenges, setbacks or opportunities.

Research by Carol Dweck (2006) suggested there are two types of mindset that people tend to have: a fixed mindset or a growth mindset.

KEY TERMS

Fixed mindset: In a fixed mindset we believe that our own and others' intelligence, personal qualities, skills and abilities are fixed and predetermined.

Growth mindset: In a growth mindset, we believe that our skills, qualities and abilities can be improved and cultivated through effort. We believe that we, and other people, can change and grow through experience. We believe that success comes as a result of hard work, effort and perseverance.

Typical thoughts and phrases of an individual with a fixed mindset include:

- 'I'm no good at maths.'
- 'I can't do DIY.'
- 'I'm brilliant at driving.'
- 'I give up.'
- 'I won't be able to do this.'
- 'I don't have a brain for languages.'
- 'I'll never be able to ride a bicycle.'
- 'I'll never get any better at this. I won't bother trying again.'
- 'I got really bad feedback. This obviously isn't for me.'
- 'I'll avoid that. I'll only fail anyway.'
- 'I'm good at this. I don't need to try hard.'

Typical thoughts and phrases used by individuals with a growth mindset include:

- 'I can get better at this.'
- 'I can't do this yet.'

- 'I'm still learning how to do this.'

- 'I've improved at this.'

- 'I've learned from my mistakes.'

- 'This could be a challenge.'

- 'I'm going to try hard at this.'

- 'I can try another way.'

- 'It's OK to make mistakes; that's how we learn.'

- 'I can keep trying.'

- 'I can learn from this experience.'

- 'I like a challenge.'

Mindsets are changeable. Simply by learning about the types of mindset, we can begin to identify our own thought patterns and our personal reactions to challenges and learning. Individuals can also have different types of mindset in different domains; for example, a person might have a fixed mindset about their ability to do maths, but adopt a growth mindset when it comes to cooking.

The benefits of a growth mindset

Adopting a growth mindset can bring many advantages. A growth mindset means an individual is open to new challenges, opportunities and possibilities, whereas in a fixed mindset a person avoids challenges and opportunities to learn. In a growth mindset a person learns from mistakes; in a fixed mindset they tend to rationalise failure. Individuals with a fixed mindset are more likely to experience stress and feel overwhelmed by increasing pressures or changes. They believe their abilities are fixed and do not expect that they will be able to overcome challenges. Those with a fixed mindset are more likely to have low self-confidence and are more likely to give up if they do not reach their goals (Dweck 2006). A growth mindset involves letting go of self-limiting beliefs that we might have about what we can't do or are no good at. Some of these beliefs might stem back to our schooldays when the focus was on passing examinations and getting things 'right' (Blyth 2013).

Goal-setting

Having a growth mindset is also linked to the idea of goal-setting. In a growth mindset individuals are more likely to set goals and feel that they are able to work towards them effectively. In a fixed mindset, individuals may avoid setting themselves goals, particularly ones that are new or they feel they might fail at. There is evidence that training in goal-setting increases feelings of wellbeing (MacLeod, Coates and Hetherton 2008), and some of the activities that follow focus on this.

> **NOTE!** We often develop resilience and a growth mindset by dealing with situations and setbacks independently – this gives us faith in our own abilities and a sense that we can deal with what happens to us in life. Too much reliance on others can lead to a 'learned helplessness', in which we believe we are incapable of solving our own problems. Ensure that group members are encouraged to act with as much independence as possible, while still receiving the support they need.

POSITIVE COPING: PUTTING IT INTO PRACTICE
Individual activities

The following activities are designed for individuals on the autism spectrum to work through independently. There is no 'right way' to complete these activities. You might like to write, draw, type, make a collage or simply think about your answers. Professionals working on a one-to-one basis with individuals on the autism spectrum might also like to guide their clients through some of these. Many activities are designed to be used as a starting point for further discussion and deeper exploration.

BALANCED REFLECTIONS

Aim: To realise that a 'bad' day might have had positive elements, and to gain a more balanced view of events.

How to do it: If can be easy for all of us to focus on the negatives at times and to believe that these were more significant than they actually were. Try this activity to help you to achieve a more balanced view of events.

1. If you feel a particular day or week has not gone so well, try splitting your day or week up into small events and list them. Example:

   Journey to work

   Team meeting

   Shelf stacking

   Lunch break

   Work on the tills

   Journey home

   Going swimming

2. Now highlight each event. Use one colour if you think that element went well, and another for things that did not go so well.

3. For each thing that went well, think about why it went well and what you enjoyed.

4. For each element that did not go so well, consider what you have learned from the experience and if there is anything you could do differently next time.

5. You will be able to see that even if small things do not go so well, it is still possible to have a good day overall.

MY ACHIEVEMENTS

Aim: To help you to recognise your achievements, both big and small.

How to do it:

1. Achievements can be big or small. Try making a list of all of your achievements to date. Remember to include:

   - Having achieved a certain goal such as a qualification, passing a driving test or other goal you have set yourself

   - Having learned a new skill such as how to swim, fix a computer or knit

   - Having improved at something you weren't so good at previously such as public speaking, using a computer, running or starting conversations

   - Gaining confidence in using a skill or in new situations

   - Trying something new for the first time

   - Persevering with something you have found difficult

   - Bouncing back from a less-than-positive experience

   - Doing something to the best of your ability, such as looking after a pet, trying hard at a job or being organised

2. Keep adding to your achievements list, maybe at the end of each week or month. Use it as a reminder of the things you have done well and improved at. Remember to identify exactly what it was that you did to contribute to the situation – did you learn something new, do something differently or act on feedback?

LEARNING FROM SUCCESS AND FAILURE

Aim: To show how you can learn from both success and perceived failure.

How to do it: You might have heard people say that you can learn from failure, but we don't always view success in the same way. However, taking some time to reflect on why we were successful means we can identify skills and strategies that we can put into place in future situations to improve outcomes.

1. Make a list of three things that have been successful for you, such as having completed a project, learned something new or achieved a goal; it might be that a meeting went well or you coped well with an unusual situation.

2. Now identify exactly what it was that you did to help this situation come about. Maybe you planned or prepared something in advance, maybe you did something differently, or maybe you used a new resource. Remember these things and think about how you could use them again. Example:

    'I had a stress-free journey to my hospital appointment today. I checked the train timetables in advance, got an earlier train to ensure I was there on time, took a book to read on the train and looked at a map to make sure I knew where to go once I got off the train. In the lobby, I asked for directions to the right department.'

3. Now consider some things that have not gone so well. Perhaps you had a negative experience or were easily put off something. Maybe you felt that something you tried 'failed' or was less successful. For each thing, consider what you learned from the situation and if there were any hidden positives. Example:

'I wasn't successful in getting a promotion I applied for at work. At the time, I was very disappointed. However, looking back, it inspired me to apply for a job elsewhere, which I now enjoy even more.'

4. Try to get into this habit of learning from both the positive and less positive experiences in life.

FROM COMFORT ZONE TO STRETCH ZONE

Aim: To identify how to move from your 'comfort zone' to your 'stretch zone'.

How to do it: Psychologists suggest that we all have a 'comfort zone' (where we feel confident and competent) and a 'stretch zone'. The stretch zone lies just outside of our normal, comfortable environment. Here we have to stretch ourselves a little more to try new things and do things that we find difficult. Gradually, these things will then become easier and our 'comfort zone' will expand to include more of these things. In our 'stretch zone' things are not impossible or overwhelming (that is our 'panic zone') but they do feel different.

1. Identify any limiting beliefs you have that are preventing you from moving into your stretch zone. Be as specific as you can. Example:

   'I don't do any sport because I am so bad at it.'

2. We all have limiting beliefs, but these are not necessarily true. They have often come about because of previous experiences or because of the attitude of those around us. Try asking yourself: 'What have been the exceptions to this?' 'Has this always been true?' 'What evidence do I have that this isn't true?' Now try to reformulate your limiting belief in light of these answers. Example:

'I was not very good at team sports in PE lessons at school, so I have avoided sport ever since. However, I have not tried many sports as an adult and when I did try running I quite enjoyed it. Maybe I am more suited to individual sports.'

3. Once you have identified the specifics, try creating an action plan to help you move from your comfort zone (in this example, doing no sport) to your stretch zone. Example:

'I could go for a walk by myself.'

'I could go swimming in the local sports centre.'

'When I am at the sports centre I could get a list of classes and could ask to be shown around the fitness suite.'

'I could try out some classes until I find one that I enjoy.'

USING SUPPORT EFFECTIVELY

Aim: To identify where you can get support.

How to do it: There will always be times when for various things you need support from another person or an organisation. Sometimes you might just need information about how things work but at other times you might need to speak to somebody or have some specific mentoring. Let's consider some of the places you can get support:

- Your local medical centre or GP surgery can help with anything medically related or illnesses, accidents and injuries.

- The NHS (National Health Service) website provides information about health, fitness, illness, pregnancy and sexual health matters.

- The local JobCentre or the JobCentre website cam give support with finding and applying for work and for help with the 'Access to Work' scheme.

- The National Autistic Society (NAS) has a detailed website about autism and lots of downloadable resources about how it might affect you. There is also guidance on autism and employment.

- Local autism agencies offer advice and information about autism. Many also offer support groups or workshops – look to see what is available in your local area.

- The Citizens Advice Bureau (CAB) offices and website provide a range of information on employment, benefits, housing, family, health, money and the law.

- The Money Advice Service provides information about money, budgeting and debt.

- The Gov.uk website offers information about government services, work, benefits, the law, driving, passports, money, tax and pensions, among other things.

- Charities and other organisations can also offer support on specific issues.

1. Look at some of the organisations listed above. More details can be found in the 'Further Reading and Resources' section of this book. Look also at what else is available in your local geographic area. In addition, you might have trusted friends, family, relatives or colleagues whom you can talk to or ask for advice.

2. Consider how you communicate best. Some people are more confident emailing, talking on the telephone or talking face-to-face. You might find it useful to take a notebook with you to meetings and note down the important points.

Alternatively, take a friend or family member. Write down the questions you want to ask in advance, and get the name and contact details of who you speak to, in case something else comes up afterwards.

COPING IN THE WORKPLACE

Aim: To identify your workplace strengths and find strategies for overcoming things you find more difficult.

How to do it:

1. Begin by making yourself a 'work profile'. Try to make some notes under each of the following headings:

    - My qualifications

    - My skills

    - My strengths

    - My previous employment/work experience

    - Work environments that suit me

    - Work environments that do not suit me

    - Things I find difficult in the workplace

    - Successful coping strategies I have developed for the workplace

    - Factors that have contributed to successful experiences of the workplace in the past

2. Consider what you have written and your current situation. If you are not currently employed, you could use your notes to help you consider which sorts of jobs and working environments you think best suit you. You might wish to discuss your thoughts with your work coach or

mentor and begin developing a CV (resumé). If you are currently employed but feel you would be better suited to working elsewhere, consider exactly what it is that is causing concern in your current role. The more accurate you can be, the easier it will be to find something that suits you better. Do you want to spend more time working independently? Do you wish to learn new skills? Could you put your current skills to better use? Are relationships with colleagues or your manager difficult? Pinpointing the exact difficulties or concerns will inform your next steps. The 'Access to Work' scheme in the UK might be one way of supporting you in employment.

3. If you feel you have difficulties in the workplace or that there are misunderstandings due to your autism, you will often need to be proactive in resolving these issues. Your colleagues and managers might not know enough about autism, or about you as an individual, to help you in the most effective way. Begin by identifying specifically what the issues are. Rather than listing 'I'm unhappy at work', try to be more exact (e.g. 'I feel anxious about being asked to cover the reception desk because I am not confident speaking on the phone'). The National Autistic Society has put together a workplace handbook for autistic individuals, which is available on their website (see 'Further Reading and Resources').

4. You might need to discuss your concerns with your line manager, the Human Resources (HR) department, or a workplace mentor. Find out who would be best to speak to and make an appointment with them. Spend some time preparing – consider your specific concerns and come up with some possible solutions that you think might work. This will make it easier for others to help you. Example:

'I really enjoy my job but I am having real trouble being productive in the noisy office environment because of the sensory overload. Would it be possible for me to have a desk in a quieter corner instead? Alternatively, are there any opportunities for me to be able to work from home for some time during the week?'

5. Employers are often busy people and they will want to see that you are aware of your autism and that you are willing to develop coping strategies to help you. Rather than just listing problems, try out various coping strategies and identify possible solutions to discuss with your employer.

THE EQUALITY ACT (2010)

Autism is a condition that is recognised as a disability under the Equality Act (2010) in the UK. This means that you should not be treated unfairly because of your autism, and that your employer should make 'reasonable adjustments' to meet your needs. If you feel you are not being treated fairly, or you need reasonable adjustments, begin by speaking to your mentor (if you have one), HR department or line manager. If you are a member of a trade union, it can offer advice and support in times of difficulty.

DISCLOSURE

You might decide to disclose your autism to your employer. You do not have to do this, if you do not want your employer to know about your autism, but you will need to disclose if you want to ask for reasonable adjustments. It is up to you if you disclose, and you can disclose at any time during the application process or once you are in a role.

Some of the benefits of disclosure:

• You do not have to hide your autism or differences.

• Others might be more understanding of your differences.

- You can ask for reasonable adjustments if you need to.

- Employers are legally required to support you and make reasonable adjustments.

Some of the potential disadvantages:

- You might not want others to know about your autism.

- Disclosure does not guarantee that others will be more understanding; there may be prejudice or stereotypical assumptions made.

- You might not want others to treat you any differently.

- You might not feel you need reasonable adjustments or that your autism affects your work.

COMMUNICATING ASSERTIVELY

Aim: To understand the difference between aggressive, passive and assertive communication skills.

How to do it: You might have heard people talk about being assertive, but just what exactly does it mean?

When we respond to a situation, we can usually respond in one of three ways: aggressively, assertively or passively.

An aggressive response can involve anger, violence and physical or verbal attacks. It might include sarcasm or attempt to hurt the other person in some way. An aggressive response does not respect other people and may include shouting, swearing, threatening or acting as if you are better than others.

A passive response often involves saying or doing nothing. It lacks confidence and avoids the problem. A passive response involves keeping your feelings to yourself and allowing others to treat you with disrespect. You may speak quietly, say nothing, make yourself look small, go along with things you are uncomfortable with, or act as if you are not as important as other people.

An assertive response, however, is in the middle of these two extremes. It involves expressing your thoughts and feelings honestly and openly. It respects both yourself and the other person and allows you to exercise your personal rights without denying the rights of others.

Individuals who are assertive are generally more able to resolve conflict, take control of their own life, be more confident in their ability to achieve, make more positive choices, and say 'no' to peer pressure. They are also less likely to be victims of aggression or bullying.

TIPS ON BEING ASSERTIVE

- Keep calm and use a low, clear and steady voice. Stand up tall and still.

- Look at the other person to show you are listening to their point of view.

- Use 'I' statements to describe how you feel (e.g. 'I feel...when you...because...'; 'I would like...').

- Respect your own feelings and those of other people.

- Do not feel that you have to keep justifying your reasons; just remain polite and firm.

- Being assertive can take practice, but it is a useful skill to master as it can help to reduce anxiety and worry.

1. Note down any examples of when you might have responded to a situation aggressively or passively. Do you have a tendency to react in a certain way? Think about examples when communicating with friends, as well as with colleagues, professionals or others.

2. Next, try to think of a way you could respond to the same situation more assertively. It can sometimes be helpful to write it down, rehearse it aloud or ask a trusted friend or family member how it sounds. Example:

   Perhaps a group of your friends enjoy going out to nightclubs, partying all night and staying out late, but this is just not your thing. You do not enjoy these situations and feel uncomfortable, but you do not like to say 'no' to your friends, so worry about the night out for the whole week, do not enjoy the evening and afterwards wish you had stayed home. When you try to say that you do not want to go, you feel as if your friends continue to pressure you into it.

   A more assertive response to this situation might be: 'Thank you for inviting me, but nightclubbing just isn't really my thing. I feel quite frustrated when you keep on trying to persuade me to join in because I know I will go away and worry about it. I do hope you enjoy the evening though.' This way you have remained polite, and respected their feelings and your own. A good follow-up could be to make a suggestion that perhaps the following week you could go to the cinema one evening or do an activity that you enjoy more. That way you are still able to spend some time with your friends but are not stopping them from doing things they enjoy.

3. Next time the situation occurs, try to use a more assertive response. How did you feel about this and what was the result?

WHAT DO YOU HAVE CONTROL OVER?

Aim: To develop resilience by identifying the elements of an issue that you have control over.

How to do it:

1. At times it can feel like we have no control over a situation and that there is nothing we can do to improve things. Consider the situation you feel negatively about or feel 'trapped' in. Examples:

    'I am stuck in a house share with a house mate I dislike and I have no other options about where to move. I can't afford to live anywhere else.'

    'I feel trapped in my job. I need to stay for a year to get the experience to move on. I dislike it because it takes over my life, I dislike my colleagues and I find the role boring.'

2. There are some things that we have no control over (e.g. the personality and behaviour of other people), but there are other elements that we can control. Try to identify these. Examples:

    'I don't have to socialise with my house mate outside of the house. I can control the environment in my own bedroom. I dislike the fact that my house mate leaves mouldy food in the fridge, and this is something we can negotiate. I can also look at other house share websites in case anywhere else comes up in the future.'

    'I can ask for new experiences at work and ask to shadow senior colleagues to give me more insight into their roles. I don't have to socialise with my colleagues – I could go for a walk at lunchtime instead, or I might have time to use the swimming pool next door. I could ask if there are opportunities for flexi-time and to start and finish earlier as this would give me a better work–life balance.'

3. You might not be successful with all of your ideas, but there are usually more elements that you have control over than you might think at first.

Group activities

The following activities are designed for professionals to deliver with groups of individuals on the autism spectrum. Again, they are not prescriptive and should be adapted according to the ages, abilities and experiences of individuals in the group. Professionals might also wish to use some of the 'individual activities' with their clients.

FIXED OR GROWTH MINDSET?

Aim: For group members to understand the difference between a 'fixed mindset' and a 'growth mindset'.

How to do it:

1. Explain to the group what is meant by a fixed mindset (when we believe our skills, abilities and traits are fixed) and a growth mindset (when we believe our skills, abilities and traits can be developed and improved through our own effort). Point out at this point that we might have a fixed mindset about some things and a growth mindset about others.

2. Give out the statements that can be found in Appendix B. These can be cut up and shuffled. Give one set to each small group or pair. Alternatively, you might prefer to divide them equally amongst the group members and take feedback as a group.

3. Allow 5–10 minutes for the small groups or pairs to discuss and categorise these statements into 'fixed mindset' and 'growth mindset'.

4. Take feedback at the end of the activity to ensure that group members have understood the difference.

5. The feedback can also be a time to begin discussion and invite group members to share any examples from their own life when they find they experience a fixed or growth mindset.

WHAT IS RESILIENCE?

Aim: For group members to understand what is meant by the term 'resilience'.

How to do it:

1. Ask the group to come up with a definition of 'resilience'. Try to facilitate the discussion so that the idea of 'bouncing back' is suggested, or learning from negative and difficult experiences to cope more effectively in the future.

2. Choose some of the scenarios from the list below. You might wish to adapt some of these so that they are more relevant for the particular group you are working with.

   • You apply for a job but do not get an interview.

   • You are studying towards a qualification and do not pass an assignment.

   • You ask somebody out on a date and they say 'no'.

   • You ask some friends if they would like to go to the cinema, but they do not seem interested.

- Your computer breaks and you lose all the work you had saved on it.

- You would like to join a sports club, but everybody looks more experienced and as if they already know each other.

- Your best friend moves to a different area.

- You are working on a temporary contract and you find out it is not going to be renewed.

3. Decide whether the group will work as a whole group, in smaller groups or in pairs. Give time for discussion of a resilient response to the situation and a less resilient response. Example:

Situation: You are working on a temporary contract and you find out it is not going to be renewed.

Resilient response: You feel upset that you will have to find a new job but accept the situation. You sign up to some job websites and look for jobs being advertised in your local newspapers. You ask your employer if they will write you a reference and you update your CV.

Less resilient response: You are upset that your contract is not being renewed and think it is very unfair. You think you will never find a new job. You do not attempt to look for a new job and do not consider doing any voluntary work or work experience. You spend a lot of time moaning about not having a job and think that your life is going to be terrible.

4. Take feedback from various situations and emphasise some of the characteristics of a resilient response, such as taking positive actions, learning from experience and not letting one negative experience affect every aspect of your life.

RECOGNISING ACHIEVEMENTS

Aim: To support group members to recognise what they have already done well and their positive achievements to date.

How to do it:

1. Explain that we have all had things that we have done well in our life. These achievements can be big or small and can include:

    -   Having achieved a certain goal such as a qualification, passing a driving test or other goal we have set ourselves

    -   Having learned a new skill, such as how to swim, fix a computer or knit

    -   Having improved at something we weren't so good at previously, such as public speaking, using a computer, running or starting conversations

    -   Gaining confidence in using skills or being in new situations

    -   Trying something new for the first time

    -   Persevering with something we have found difficult

    -   Bouncing back from a less-than-positive experience

    -   Doing something to the best of our ability, such as looking after a pet, trying hard at a job or being organised

2. Ask group members to generate a list of some of their experiences. Some might find this difficult, so will benefit from working with a supportive friend or professional helping with the group.

3. When taking feedback, invite each group member to share an achievement they feel proud of. When facilitating feedback, try to focus on the individual's actions in helping this situation to come about, rather than these 'achievements' being things that 'just happened' to them. Example:

   Rather than 'I got more confident speaking to new people', try to elicit specifics such as 'I tried hard at chatting to new people, even though I found it scary' or 'I made the effort to chat to one new person each day when I was doing work experience in a shop.'

4. You might like to suggest to some individuals who have found this difficult that they try keeping an 'achievement diary' and note down their achievements, big and small, over the next few weeks.

BOUNCING BACK

Aim: To identify positives from a situation that might appear 'negative' at the time.

How to do it:

1. Explain how sometimes things do not go to plan, but we can learn and develop from these experiences. You might like to give some examples; for example, how Post-It® notes were developed by Dr Silver Spencer when he was actually intending to create a super-strong adhesive for use in airplanes; or the New York donut seller who reportedly found his baked goods were raw in the middle – he simply scooped out these parts and so the ring donut was created!

2. Invite group members to share any examples from their own experiences of a situation or event they thought had 'gone wrong' at the time but actually ended up having

a positive outcome. Examples might include having experienced a disappointment (such as not getting a job) but then having found a positive (a job was then found that was closer to home).

3. Now ask if any group members would like to share any situations or events that they currently perceive as less positive. Encourage other group members to suggest possible positives that could be found in the situation or more helpful ways of viewing the situation.

4. Following this, some individuals might need support in putting some future actions into place.

DEVELOPING A GROWTH MINDSET

Aim: To support group members to identify situations that they would like to approach more positively or with a growth mindset, and put together an action plan.

How to do it:

1. Ask group members to identify a situation that they feel they currently approach with a fixed mindset. Example:

    'I will never be able to get a job.'

2. Explain to the group that we can all hold limiting beliefs and that these beliefs are not necessarily true. Ask group members to identify the beliefs they hold that contribute to their fixed mindset. Examples:

    'I applied for two jobs but was not successful.'

    'Other people have more qualifications and experience than me.'

    'I wasn't very good at working with others when I was in school.'

3. Now ask your group members to challenge each of their beliefs. In some groups, participants might be able to work in pairs and challenge each other. They could ask themselves, or each other, 'What evidence do you have against this belief?' Examples:

'I had a job in a small café that I enjoyed a few years ago, but the café closed down.'

'I am good at working with others when I play in a band at the weekend.'

4. Some participants might need this broken down further into smaller questions, such as 'Has there ever been a time when things were different?' 'Has there ever been a time you felt more positively about this situation?'

5. Participants could also ask, 'What advice would you give a friend in this situation?' Examples:

'There are plenty of jobs that do not require experience.'

'You could go to college to learn something new.'

'You could do some volunteer work or work experience to gain new skills.'

6. Once participants have begun to think about their situation differently, ask them to create an action plan of steps they will put into place to help them to develop a growth mindset relating to this situation. Some group members might need support to put these steps into place.

GETTING SUPPORT

Aim: To show group members where they can find support to help them in various situations.

How to do it:

1. Explain to the group that we all might need support from others at times to help us cope with various circumstances. That is why support organisations exist.

2. Start by giving some examples of situations where individuals might need support. Which organisations available locally would be best to approach? This can be a way of identifying which organisations are known to your group and where, if anywhere, help is already being sought. Ask about the following situations and add others that are relevant to your group:

    - Finding something in the workplace difficult

    - Needing help finding a job

    - Wanting to discuss your thoughts and feelings

    - A medical issue

    - Not understanding which benefits you are entitled to

    - Wanting to understand more about how your autism affects you

    - Needing support sorting a housing problem

    - Wanting to become more involved in your local community

    - Wanting to learn a specific skill, such as improved communication skills

    - Needing support studying towards a qualification

3. During the feedback, introduce your group to the organisations, services and charities that offer support in your local area. It can be helpful to give out leaflets and contact details of these organisations. Remember that

some individuals on the autism spectrum might have preferred methods of communication, such as preferring to communicate via email rather than by phone. You can also signpost group members to national organisations (e.g. the Samaritans or the Citizens Advice Bureau) or websites as well as local organisations and autism-specific organisations.

4. Depending on your group you might decide to follow this up in the following ways:

- Invite representatives of these organisations to come and introduce themselves and their services.

- Visit local services, such as the local Citizens Advice Bureau (CAB) so that group members know where to find these places.

- Role-play different situations in which individuals are trying to find support with different things.

USING CARTOONS TO HELP

Aim: To use a cartoon strip to help to understand why a misunderstanding has occurred and to develop positive strategies for the future.

How to do it: 'Comic Strip Conversations' were originally developed by Carol Gray for use with individuals on the autism spectrum. Full details can be found in Carol Gray's books and through resources listed at the end of this book. This activity adapts a comic strip conversation for more general use in a group situation.

1. Consider a situation, event or misunderstanding that has occurred for your group members. If might be a specific

incident that a group member would like support with, or a more general one that has occurred for several group members. For some groups or individuals it might work best to 'depersonalise' this activity by using a 'superhero' or comic book character instead of talking about a specific individual.

2. Draw this on paper, a board or a flip chart as a cartoon strip. Use any group members with creative talents to help.

3. Once the situation has been split into 'scenes' and drawn, add speech bubbles for what was said and discuss the misunderstanding or 'negative' experience. Next add in thought bubbles to see if group members can identify what people might have been thinking. This can sometimes help to see different perspectives and points of view.

4. See if group members can identify now where the misunderstanding might occur. Some situations might not be clear-cut. There is not always a 'right' point of view – merely different ones that sometimes have to be expected.

5. Finally, cartoon or role-play an alternative version of events in which the situation is handled more effectively to avoid misunderstandings. Role-playing can also be a way of rehearsing communication and assertiveness skills. Suggest more effective ways of acting when this situation occurs again in the future.

CREATING WORK PROFILES

Aim: For each group member to create a 'work profile' that will help them to identify their workplace skills and overcome any difficulties they face.

How to do it:

1. Group members might like to complete this on paper or on a computer. Ask each group member to make some notes under the following headings:

    - My qualifications

    - My skills

    - My previous employment experiences

    - My strengths

    - Things I can find difficult in the workplace due to my Asperger's/autism

    - Successful strategies I use to overcome these difficulties

2. Some individuals might need more support than others to answer these questions and to identify their strengths and skills.

3. When taking the feedback, concentrate on the successful strategies that individuals are using. Other members of the group might like to try some of these out or adapt them for themselves. Show group members that employers will not want to have a list of all the things they find difficult but to know how the individual is taking proactive steps to empower themselves, and how they can help as an employer. Example:

    'I know I sometimes find it difficult to eliminate background noise in a busy office, but if I can work in a quiet corner then I can get more done. I also sometimes wear ear defenders, which helps me.'

4. Individuals within the group might like to use these documents as a basis for discussion with their work coach or as a basis for compiling a CV.

7

WELLBEING

WELLBEING: THE THEORY

The word 'wellbeing' is often used and can mean different things. 'Physical wellbeing' is made up of a number of components – diet, physical activity, energy levels, sleep quality, physical health. 'Emotional and mental wellbeing' refers to how we feel at a general, everyday level – Do we have an overall sense of being able to cope? Do we generally feel positive about ourselves and our life?

The two aspects of physical and mental wellbeing are closely linked. If you have ever suffered from a lack of sleep you will know how much more difficult it is to cope when you feel exhausted. Small, everyday challenges can seem insurmountable, and over-tiredness can lead to lack of concentration, lack of enthusiasm and increased irritability. Individuals who exercise regularly have also been shown to have a reduced risk of depression (Mayor 2017).

Previous chapters have already suggested many activities that can be put into place to support mental wellbeing levels. This chapter considers physical wellbeing, as well as further strategies to support emotional wellbeing levels.

Physical wellbeing and autism

There can sometimes be some specific challenges for individuals on the autism spectrum in achieving a sense of physical wellbeing, although it is worth remembering that many of these can also affect the general population too.

Sleep

- Sensory sensitivities can play a role. Some individuals on the autism spectrum might be particularly sensitive to noise or light, or may prefer a weighted blanket.

- Individuals on the autism spectrum might experience a constant high level of anxiety. They might find it difficult to sleep as they are ruminating on worries and concerns.

- Unhealthy lifestyle habits that impact the general population will also affect those on the autism spectrum. Individuals may have their sleep interrupted by mobile phones, or spend evenings watching television or using digital devices – screen exposure before bedtime has been shown to disrupt sleep.

Exercise

- Some people may have been discouraged from sport due to the emphasis on team games when they were at school. Individuals on the autism spectrum can find it difficult to communicate with others during team sports, and close proximity to other people might increase anxiety levels. Instructions and rules may also be difficult to follow in team sports.

- Motor skills can be difficult for some individuals on the autism spectrum. Some might find it difficult to throw or catch a ball, to use sports equipment, or to move fluently and comfortably. Some individuals, therefore, may find some sports uncomfortable, or feel embarrassed exercising around others.

- Sensory issues can play a role. Some individuals may feel uncomfortable in certain sports clothing or using certain sports equipment. Gyms and sports centres can sometimes be noisy environments with too much sensory input.

- Other issues that can discourage the general population from exercise can also be difficult for those on the autism spectrum.

Poor body image, feeling embarrassed, not wanting to use communal changing rooms, preferring other activities, lacking confidence might all be contributory factors.

Healthy eating

- Sensory sensitivities can impact healthy eating. Some individuals on the autism spectrum may be particularly averse to certain tastes, smells or textures.

- Some individuals on the autism spectrum may be unwilling to try new foods, or prefer to eat the same meals, prepared in the same way, every day.

- For some individuals on the autism spectrum, the social nature of mealtimes can be overwhelming; others might prefer to eat in the company of family or peers (National Autistic Society 2016b).

- There is some evidence that individuals on the autism spectrum may be more likely to experience eating disorders than the rest of the population (Gillberg, Råstam and Gillberg 1995). Individuals on the autism spectrum may be particularly susceptible because of low self-esteem, high anxiety, a need to have control over their life, a reliance on routine, interpreting language literally, and fixed thinking habits. Sensory issues can also play a role, as can being particularly focused on numbers and patterns (e.g. counting calories, weight, measurements).

Sensory sensitivities

Many individuals on the autism spectrum experience sensory sensitivities; this means that they may be over- or under-sensitive to certain sensory stimuli (e.g. lights, noise, textures, tastes, smells, touch). When autistic individuals are overwhelmed by sensory input, they can experience increased anxiety, making it difficult to think and concentrate. They may become less able to communicate and this can sometimes result in 'shut-down' (becoming extremely withdrawn and having to isolate themselves), or in 'melt-down' (a temporary loss of behavioural control due to being overwhelmed by the current situation – this could include shouting, crying or lashing out). Being overwhelmed by sensory input is not only extremely uncomfortable for autistic individuals, but can also be physically painful. Many everyday environments, such as shops, workplaces and community facilities, can be overwhelming with their noises, visuals, crowds, smells and lights. Some individuals might find themselves in a constant state of anxiety and discomfort.

Emotional wellbeing

As well as strategies already covered in this book, there are many other activities that have been shown to increase wellbeing levels.

- Being outdoors and spending time in nature has been shown to have a positive impact on wellbeing – this can include time walking, gardening, or simply being in nature (Mechelli 2018).

- Keeping a journal has been found to increase happiness levels (Roberts 2015) as this can help us to make sense of feelings and to reflect on thoughts, emotions and events.

- Reading has been shown to have many wellbeing benefits. One report suggests that regular readers are less likely to experience depression than non-readers, and that one in five readers have been inspired by books to make positive changes in their life (Reading Agency 2016). Other studies show that reading helps us to develop empathy by enabling us to get inside the minds of other people and see things from different perspectives (Bergland 2014).

- Studies show that crafting, such as knitting, sewing and crocheting, can have a positive impact on happiness and wellbeing. It is thought that spending time engaged in these activities can increase feelings of 'flow' or a meditative state (McKay 2014).

- There is also evidence that spending time with pets and animals can increase human wellbeing levels (Wells 2011).

- Spending time on social media is often associated with lowered levels of wellbeing. This is thought to be because users begin to compare their own life with the 'edited highlights' that others have shared. Constant exposure to images of others with more privileged lifestyles has been shown to increase unhappiness and a sense of loneliness in young people (Blanden 2006). Online comments can also appear superficial, and some people can feel stressed because of the discrepancy between the public persona they present to the world and their internal insecurities (Gardner and Davis 2013). There is also evidence that being constantly connected to digital devices means our brains do not get the restorative 'down-time' they need to promote wellbeing and be able to focus effectively when needed (Carr 2010).

WELLBEING: PUTTING IT INTO PRACTICE
Individual activities

The following activities are designed for individuals on the autism spectrum to work through independently. There is no 'right way' to complete these activities. You might like to write, draw, type, make a collage or simply think about your answers. Professionals working on a one-to-one basis with individuals on the autism spectrum might also like to guide their clients through some of these. Many of these activities can be used as a starting point for further discussion and deeper exploration.

INCREASING WELLBEING

Aim: To identify ways you could further increase your wellbeing levels.

How to do it:

1. Consider the following list of activities, which have been shown to improve wellbeing. Consider which, if any, you think you could benefit from. Set aside time to include more of these into your daily routine.

    - **Sleep:** We all need sufficient good quality sleep to function optimally. Do you feel you sleep well at night? Do you have a regular bedtime routine? Try going to bed at a set time each night and turning off screens an hour before you go to sleep. Ensure that the physical environment of your bedroom is calm and conducive to sleeping well. If you have significant difficulties sleeping, consult a health professional.

    - **Exercise:** Physical activity has been shown to improve physical, mental and emotional health. Do you feel you exercise enough? Could you try out any new sports, or incorporate more walking, cycling or swimming into your day?

    - **Healthy eating:** Eating well can also contribute to both physical and mental health. Do you eat a balanced and varied diet? Are there food groups you need to eat more of or eat in moderation? If you are worried about eating a healthy diet, or if you feel you are suffering an eating disorder, speak to a health professional.

    - **Spending time outdoors:** Being in nature has also been shown to have various benefits for our health and wellbeing. Do you spend time outdoors? Perhaps you enjoy walking, cycling, rowing or running? Maybe you like to walk the dog, or visit forests, woods, mountains or the coast? Perhaps you have a garden or an allotment you enjoy working in? There are many ways of spending more time in nature – think about what works for you.

- **Journalling:** Some people find that keeping a journal or diary helps them to make sense of their thoughts and feelings. See if this works for you too.

- **Reading:** There are many non-fiction and self-help books that can be sources of advice and inspiration. Fiction can also be a way of finding out about other places and other people's perspectives. Try joining your local library and find books you enjoy.

- **Crafting and other hobbies:** Activities that require focus and concentration also add to wellbeing levels. Are there any activities that you enjoy, such as crafting, sewing, knitting, card-making, woodwork, metalwork, drawing, painting, pottery?

MY SENSORY PROFILE

Aim: To gain a deeper insight into any sensory preferences and reduce the distress these may cause

How to do it: Humans have five main senses: sight, sound, smell, touch and texture. Everybody – not just people on the autism spectrum – has different sensory preferences and tolerances.

It is usual to have sensory likes and dislikes. Some of these dislikes might even be quite intense; for example, plenty of people hate sprouts, or find the smell of sweaty shoes particularly putrid! It is also perfectly usual for different people to have different sensory tolerances; for example, some people like to listen to very loud music, while others prefer a lower volume when listening to music or watching television.

Some people on the autism spectrum also experience specific sensory sensitivities. This is where sensory input is so intense that it can feel incredibly uncomfortable and even painful. This is called being 'hyper-sensitive' (or over-sensitive). Other people on the autism spectrum can experience the opposite and may be 'hypo-sensitive' (under-sensitive) to sensory input; for example, they can be completely oblivious to smells, or may not be sensitive to taste. This hypo-sensitivity can also have its downsides – the individual might not recognise when they have body odour, or might eat non-food items because they are the only things that they can taste.

In addition, there are some other 'senses' that individuals on the autism spectrum might have some differences with. These can include proprioception (awareness of where your body is in space), motor skills (co-ordinating movements) and balance.

Complete the table below (it is also provided in Appendix C as a printable resource) with any sensory differences you experience.

Next, try to identify any coping strategies that you have developed, or that you could try out. Sometimes you might have to try several different things before you find what works for you. (Remember that everybody will have different preferences and will find different strategies work best.)

Sense	My differences	My coping strategies
Sight/visual		
Sound		
Smell		
Taste		
Texture		
Balance		
Motor skills		
Body awareness		

Example:

Sense	My differences	My coping strategies
Texture	Clothing feels 'scratchy and itchy' to me.	I cut out the care labels from clothes. I buy clothes made from cotton and other materials I find more comfortable. I wear a soft T-shirt underneath jumpers, . which is more comfortable. I look to see if seam-free clothes are available.

Some further ideas for successful coping strategies could include:

- Wearing headphones or ear plugs in noisy environments

- Working and meeting others in quieter environments

- Reducing any background noise where possible

- Keeping living and working areas tidy and clutter-free

- Reducing the amount of visual distractions in work or living areas

- Cutting labels out of clothing

- Choosing clothing in softer fabrics

- Using a weighted blanket

- Telling others about your need for personal space, or any dislike of physical touch

- Moving furniture and other equipment where you cannot trip over it

- Wearing glasses with tinted lenses if you find bright lights uncomfortable

- Using natural light when possible

- Using lamps or dimmer switches to create a more comfortable atmosphere

- Limiting the time you spend in overwhelming environments; visiting supermarkets at quieter times or shopping online

- Asking if you can move to a quieter area if you need to concentrate on an important conversation

SOCIAL ENERGY PLANNING

Aim: To identify your 'social energy' levels and how to work with these.

How to do it: Several researchers in the field of autism have identified that some individuals on the autism spectrum can have less 'social energy' (Rowe 2015) than their neurotypical counterparts. 'Socialising' and being around other people might leave them feeling exhausted and unable to function as well as they usually do. Does this apply to you? If so, consider whether any of the following strategies could be beneficial to you. Alternatively, you can develop your own.

- Use a diary or calendar, and if you see a week becoming very busy, try to rearrange some activities so that you get more balance.

- If you know you have a day with lots of socialising, try to plan a quieter day the following day.

- Socialise or join in activities with others for shorter periods of time – don't be afraid to leave earlier than others, or just go for a short time.

- See if you can identify any particular 'energy drainers' for you – activities that you know will sap your energy. This can help you with planning your week. Energy drainers could include lack of sleep, too many social interactions, too much sensory input, being in noisy environments, not having eaten well, not enough exercise, being worried about something, having experienced misunderstandings, trying new things, changes to routine, being around people you find difficult.

- Try to identify any 'energy boosters' – things that can help you to restore your energy levels. Some ideas might include spending time alone, being in a quiet environment, natural lighting, being outdoors, exercising, resting, sleeping, spending time on a hobby or interest, reading, talking to a trusted friend.

- Over time, learn what works for you in terms of your routine and personal needs regarding 'social energy'.

LONELINESS TOOLKIT

Aim: To have a bank of strategies to put in place if you are experiencing loneliness.

How to do it: There is a difference between 'being alone' and 'being lonely'. Many people – perhaps especially those on the autism spectrum – enjoy their own company and are happy being alone. Loneliness, however, is something different. Feeling lonely can be a negative experience for many people, particularly in the 21st century, where we can generally lack face-to-face contact with others. In addition, social media can make it seem that everybody else if having more fun than we are, and much communication takes place online while we are multi-tasking, rather than through deeper, face-to-face communication.

Take a look at the following list. Identify whether any of these strategies would be beneficial to you if you are experiencing loneliness.

- Talking to a friend or family member

- Arranging a meet-up with friends

- Going out (e.g. to the cinema, a sporting event, a museum)

- Exercising

- Taking up a new hobby

- Joining a community or special-interest group

- Volunteering your time somewhere

- Contacting your local autism support organisation and seeing what they offer

- Visiting your local community centre to see what is on

- Emailing or communicating online with a friend or family member

- Speaking confidentially to a stranger (e.g. Samaritans)

- Spending time with a pet or looking after animals

- Taking part in an activity (e.g. yoga, tai chi or meditation) that encourages you to connect with something bigger than yourself

MINDFULNESS

Aim: To explore mindfulness as a way of improving wellbeing.

How to do it: Mindfulness simply means paying attention to the present moment, rather than letting our thoughts wander back into the past (rumination) or into the future (worry). Try to notice your thoughts – do you find yourself thinking about the past or future rather than focusing on the present?

Mindfulness also includes responding non-judgementally to our thoughts. We are always going to have thoughts pop into our mind, but we do not always have to engage with them or react to them. Try to say to yourself, 'I'm having the thought that...(e.g. I'll never be any good at this) again.' Try not to judge your thoughts; just accept that they will come and go.

Begin to pay more attention to the present moment, wherever you are. What can you hear? Listen fully. What do you notice? Look for small details you have never noticed before. Eat slowly and pay attention to the taste, smell and texture of your food. Take a few moments to consider how your body is feeling and the sensations you are experiencing.

You might consider finding out more about mindfulness by attending a class or workshop. There is more information on the NHS website.

Group activities

The following activities are designed for professionals to deliver with groups of individuals on the autism spectrum. Again, they are not prescriptive and should be adapted according to the ages, abilities and experiences of individuals in the group. Professionals might also wish to use some of the 'individual activities' with their clients.

THE GOOD AND BAD OF SOCIAL MEDIA

Aim: To support group members to identify the positives and negatives of social media and how to use social media platforms more wisely.

How to do it:

1. This activity can be done in a whole group, or you might wish to divide the group into pairs or threes. Give out the

statement cards from Appendix D – one set for each small group, or distribute them around the whole group.

2. Facilitate discussion about each statement. Do group members believe this is a positive or negative aspect of social media? Ask them to create two piles. (In this activity there are no right or wrong answers. The statements are there to facilitate discussion and to enable group members to consider that each of these could be both positive and negative. Discussion is an opportunity to highlight some of the possible pitfalls of social media, such as 'fake news', the fact that people tend only to share the 'edited highlights' of their life, the ease of copying and pasting, how quickly information can be shared, and how information can be found by future employers.)

3. Once the statements have been discussed, give out the scenario cards (these can also be found in Appendix D).

4. Ask small groups, or the whole group, to discuss the best course of action in each scenario. Again, there are no right or wrong answers.

5. Use the feedback to gauge how much further input group members need on the topic of social media. Remember that some individuals might understand the issues theoretically but find it more difficult to put the action points into practice.

SENSORY PREFERENCES AND PROFILES

Aim: To support group members in identifying their sensory differences and effective coping strategies.

How to do it:

1. Explain to the group that some individuals on the autism spectrum may be under- or over-sensitive to sensory

input such as sights, sounds, tastes, textures or smell. Some may also have differences with body awareness or motor skills. Give some examples, such as having difficulty in eliminating background noise or having a tendency to stand too close to other people.

2. Ask group members to share any differences of their own. You might wish to facilitate a whole group discussion or discussion in pairs. Group members might like to make notes on the table provided in Appendix C.

3. Ask group members to share any successful coping strategies (e.g. wearing tinted lenses, meeting with friends in quieter places, moving furniture to the edges of rooms so that it is not tripped over). This can be a good time to make suggestions to group members and for them to help each other to adapt strategies for different situations and circumstances.

4. Highlight to your group that some venues and organisations are becoming specifically more 'autism-friendly'. You might like to share examples from your local area. Remind participants that if any individuals have specific difficulties in the workplace due to their sensory sensitivities, they can ask for 'reasonable adjustments' to be made.

5. Suggest that each individual in the group makes a list of strategies they wish to try out or adapt. Check back on progress at a later date.

WELLBEING CAROUSEL

Aim: To introduce group members to a range of activities that they might like to develop or continue with in order to promote better levels of wellbeing.

How to do it: How this activity is delivered will depend on your group and setting. You might wish to set up a 'carousel' of activities around a large hall or in different rooms, so that individuals can try out different things for a short while and then move on. Alternatively, you might wish to invite in experts from different fields to give short talks or taster sessions about each activity, or plan trips to local services and organisations to try things out. However you decide to arrange it, the aim is to introduce the group to a range of activities that can promote their wellbeing. You might like to include:

- **Nutrition and healthy eating:** Perhaps organise a talk, demonstration or cookery lessons, and provide examples of different foods to try.

- **Exercise:** Taster sessions for various sports could include aerobics, yoga, circuits, gym equipment, running, cycling, swimming, group exercise classes, martial arts, climbing, tennis, squash and team sports.

- **Sleep:** Organise a talk on the importance of sleep and how to improve it.

- **Reading:** A visit to a local library can introduce group members to fiction and non-fiction.

- **Mindfulness:** A taster session on mindfulness might be included.

- **Crafting:** You could include opportunities to try out new activities such as card-making, sewing, knitting, crafting, woodwork or metal work.

- **Other hobbies and interests:** You could invite representatives from local groups and organisations.

8

MEANING, PURPOSE AND CONNECTION

MEANING, PURPOSE AND CONNECTION: THE THEORY

This chapter discusses the topics of meaning, purpose and connection. We've looked at possible strategies to help improve happiness and wellbeing on an individual level, in terms of what we can do to help our bodies and our mind. This chapter looks at the 'wider' or 'bigger' issues that can contribute to us feeling fulfilled at a deeper level.

Is having meaning and purpose important?

Evidence shows that having a sense of deeper meaning and purpose in our life has many wellbeing benefits and helps us to cope in tough times (King 2017). This sort of deeper purpose is often linked to having a sense of spirituality or deeper connection with the world around us. Having meaning and purpose has been associated with a number of positive outcomes, including subjective wellbeing, health, longevity, reduced stress and resilience (LeBon 2014).

Meaning and purpose are often associated with our 'relationship with life' and it is argued that nature has hard-wired us with a strong drive to seek out and foster health-bringing relationships (Baylis 2009). These relationships do not just have to be with the people around us but can also be with the natural world of flora and fauna, between our mind and body, or between our conscious and subconscious (Baylis 2009).

Does searching for meaning and purpose have downsides?

Although having meaning and purpose in our life is generally associated with positive outcomes, it is less certain whether *searching* for meaning and purpose increases wellbeing. Some researchers suggest that deliberately searching for meaning in our life may be less beneficial (Yalom 1989), for example by increasing anxiety, over-thinking and rumination (LeBon 2014). It is similar to happiness and wellbeing: we benefit from giving ourselves a nudge in the right direction and from making time for it in our life, but if we spend too long searching, the gap between our reality and our 'ideal' might become more apparent to us, making us feel anxious and overwhelmed. Happiness, wellbeing, meaning and purpose are often by-products of other activities.

How do we find meaning and purpose?

What is meaningful is different for all of us: some may find meaning in following a specific religion; others may have a philosophy that brings meaning to their life; for some a connection with nature may be important; others have a sense of vocation or contribution to the world. Experts often identify four common sources of meaning (Esfahani Smith 2017):

- A sense of belonging (our relationships with others)

- Purpose (a feeling of contributing to the world)

- Storytelling (how we make sense of the world around us)

- Transcendence (connecting with something bigger than ourselves)

Values

Identifying our personal values can help us to seek out opportunities that are meaningful to us. Values are individual to us and we might need to consider carefully whether we are being influenced by those around us, the media, or current societal and cultural values. Research indicates that values need to be owned by the individual in order to contribute to a feeling of meaning and purpose in that person (Deci and Ryan 1985).

Meaning, purpose and autism

Identifying meaning and purpose can be just as difficult for individuals on the autism spectrum as for anybody else. What is perhaps especially important for those on the autism spectrum is that they remain authentic to themselves and learn to connect with their authentic self, rather than trying too hard to 'fit in' and be more 'neurotypical'. This is likely to lead to internal conflict and a sense of disconnection. It can also be difficult to stick to your personal values in a world designed predominantly for a different way of being. Many individuals on the autism spectrum do go on to find meaning and purpose in their life. Indeed, some would suggest that spirituality plays an important role in the life of many autistic people (Bogdashina 2013).

It is also useful to note the difference between 'being alone' and 'loneliness'. Having a sense of connection does not necessarily mean spending long periods of time socialising with others. Many individuals on the autism spectrum are happy to spend time alone and find this time enriching and restorative. They may feel happy in their own company and value the time to enjoy personal space free from interruption. 'Being alone' in this sense is a choice and one that should be respected. Indeed, the ability to be at ease in your own company is often considered to be an essential prerequisite for spiritual development, through practices such as meditation and mindfulness.

Feeling 'lonely', however, is different and can create feelings of emptiness, isolation and depression. It is important not to assume individuals on the autism spectrum are 'lonely' when they just enjoy 'being alone'. Equally, it is just as important not to assume they enjoy being alone, if they are experiencing loneliness and require support to feel connected to others.

MEANING, PURPOSE AND CONNECTION: PUTTING IT INTO PRACTICE
Individual activities

The following activities are designed for individuals on the autism spectrum to work through independently. There is no 'right way' to complete these activities. You might like to write, draw, type, make a collage or simply think about your answers. Professionals working on a one-to-one basis with individuals on the autism spectrum might also like to guide their clients through some of these. Many activities can be used as a starting point for further discussion and deeper exploration.

VALUES CLARIFIER

Aim: To become clearer about your personal values and how you could build more of your life around these.

How to do it: Identifying our values can help us to decide what is meaningful for us. Try the following activities to help you identify your values.

1. Make a list or spider diagram of all of the things that are important to you – this could include people, animals, hobbies, interests, important causes, work, lifestyle factors, spirituality, hopes for the future, or wider issues.

2. Some questions that might help you to identify your values include: 'What would your ideal day look like?' Who do you admire and why?' 'How would you like to be remembered?'

3. Use your answers to look at the examples of values below and decide which ones are your top values. Identifying

these can help you to decide which work and lifestyle activities are most meaningful to you.

- Accomplishment
- Achievement
- Adventure
- Ambition
- Art
- Awe
- Belonging
- Calmness
- Carefulness
- Challenge
- Cheerfulness
- Courage
- Creativity
- Curiosity
- Determination
- Education
- Encouragement
- Energy
- Enjoyment
- Environment
- Expertise
- Fairness
- Family
- Fashion
- Forgiveness
- Freedom
- Friendship
- Fun
- Generosity
- Hard work
- Helpfulness
- Hopefulness
- Humour
- Imagination
- Independence
- Individuality
- Integrity
- Kindness
- Knowledge
- Logic
- Making a difference
- Modesty
- Nature
- Open-mindedness

- Patience
- Religion
- Success

- Truth
- Volunteering
- Wisdom

HOW I CONNECT WITH OTHERS

Aim: To identify any specific strengths and difficulties when connecting and interacting with others.

How to do it: Often individuals on the autism spectrum can find it difficult to connect and interact with others. Perhaps it can be difficult to make friends or to find people who have shared interests and values. There might be frequent misunderstandings, or you might simply not enjoy socialising.

1. Begin by using the following prompts to reflect on how you connect with others. Add to these with examples. Reading your answers back, you might find that some patterns or insights are highlighted.

   - When do you enjoy your own company?
   - What activities do you prefer to do independently?
   - Which people do you enjoy being with?
   - When do you, or have you, felt comfortable in other people's company?
   - Who do you enjoy talking to?
   - Who do you find it easy to have a conversation with?
   - When do you find it easier to socialise?
   - When do you find it harder to socialise?
   - Which situations do you find harder?
   - How do you find communicating with strangers?

- Which conversational skills do you find more difficult?

    - Who are the people you appreciate having in your life?

2. When answering the questions above, consider all aspects of your life – colleagues at work, neighbours, friends, family members, customers/clients, acquaintances, fellow members of groups and clubs. Be as specific as you can. If you have identified any specific difficulties, see if you can identify why these misunderstandings occur. There are several books listed in the 'Further Reading and Resources' section of this book that can give you greater insight into some of the differences in interacting for individuals on the autism spectrum.

CONNECTING WITH MY COMMUNITY

Aim: To identify various ways to become more involved with your local community.

How to do it: The community around you can be a source of friendship and support. We all want different levels of involvement with our local community, and that is fine. If you would like to get more involved, consider whether any of the activities on the list below appeal to you and how you could go about getting involved in these. Having a say in your community is important, so that a range of voices and opinions, including those from individuals on the autism spectrum, are heard and taken into consideration.

Possible ways of connecting with your community:

- Joining a sports group

- Joining a group related to an interest or hobby

- Being a member of a spiritual or religious group

- Attending a class, course or workshop

- Attending local events

  - Starting up a special interest group

  - Voting in local and general elections

  - Taking an interest in your local council

  - Using local services

  - Providing feedback for local surveys gathering residents' views

  - Reporting issues such as potholes or broken street-lamps

  - Taking part in volunteer work

  - Organising a community event

MY COMMUNICATION SKILLS SELF-AUDIT

Aim: To evaluate your communication skills and identify any areas you would like to develop.

How to do it: Some individuals on the autism spectrum can have differences in the way that they communicate. Being aware of any differences can be a step towards understanding why some misunderstandings might have occurred. Communication is a two-way process, and other people might have difficulties with communication skills, too. We can't control what other people do, but if there are aspects of our own communication we would like to develop, we can do.

1. Use the self-audit in Appendix I to evaluate what you do well and whether there are areas you would like to improve. You might be able to find specific ideas by using books, looking on the internet, enquiring at an autism support organisation or speaking to a speech and language therapist.

2. You might also choose to ask a trusted friend or relative what they think your communication strengths and areas for development are. Sometimes just being aware of our communication differences and preferences can help us to face these with more balance and acceptance.

MY CAREER AND LIFESTYLE

Aim: To identify what is important to you when considering a longer-term career.

How to do it: We spend a lot of time at work so it is important that we find a role that suits us well. Some of us might not have received much careers advice in the past, and it can take us until adulthood to realise what we are best suited for. Rather than just considering the qualifications you have and which jobs they match, this activity encourages you to consider some of the wider issues.

1. Consider the following questions:

- What are you passionate about?

- What do you enjoy learning about?

- What are your hobbies and interests?

- What are your strengths and skills?

- What energises you?

- What drains your energy?

- What are your values?

- What gives your life meaning and purpose?

- Which environments do you feel most comfortable in?

- Which environments do you feel less comfortable in?

- What does work mean to you?

- What else is important in your life?

- How do you want to be remembered?

2. Consider your responses to the questions above. Do they point to a type of job you might be suited for? Consider also whether self-employment could be an option for you, or having a 'portfolio career' (i.e. earning an income from several different sources).

3. Consider what else you could do to move into a career you enjoy. Could you do voluntary work? Work shadowing? Work part-time or get a temporary job? Speak to people in a job you'd like? Attend a careers fair or business networking event?

Group activities

The following activities are designed for professionals to deliver with groups of individuals on the autism spectrum. Again, they are not prescriptive and should be adapted according to the ages, abilities and experiences of individuals in the group. Professionals might also wish to use some of the 'individual activities' with their clients.

WHAT MAKES A FRIEND?

Aim: To reflect on friendship skills.

How to do it:

1. Ask the group, 'What makes a good friend?' Depending on your setting, you might facilitate a group discussion, ask smaller groups to make a spider diagram, or ask individuals to write their thoughts on sticky notes and place them on a board.

2. Discuss the answers that have been given and explore why each of these issues are important. Try to discuss

how some aspects of friendship cannot always be taken literally (e.g. 'A friend is always there for me' – there may be times when the friend is very busy with other priorities so cannot devote as much time to the friendship).

3. Next, discuss the friendship statements that are listed below. Ask the group how far they agree or disagree. There are no right or wrong answers; it is an activity to explore what is meant by friendship.

   - All friendships last forever.

   - Friends are people you can talk to about your thoughts and feelings.

   - Good friends have to live near you.

   - A friend respects your opinions and beliefs, even if they are different to their own.

   - Friends have to be the same age as you.

   - You have to socialise with friends regularly to maintain the friendship.

   - Friends have to have the same hobbies and interests.

   - Friendships often develop slowly.

   - If a friend does not get in touch for a while, it means they no longer want to be your friend.

   - It is better to have a wide range of friends than just one.

4. Having discussed the nature of friendship and the many different forms friendship can take, discuss how friendship is a two-way process and both sides need to work at the friendship. You might use this as a way to ask if anybody has any specific difficulties with friendships, and share advice or helpful strategies.

LISTENING SKILLS

Aim: To identify any barriers to listening and to highlight the importance of listening skills.

How to do it: Being able to listen well brings many benefits. It makes it easier to get to know new people and to connect with them. It also means we are more likely to remember key points and understand what is going on. Some autistic individuals have differences in how they listen – perhaps finding eye contact uncomfortable or finding it difficult to eliminate background noise. This activity is not about changing those differences but about supporting those individuals to become aware of them, and making suggestions that could make it easier for them to listen more effectively.

1. Divide the group into pairs. One person takes on the role of the 'talker' and the other is the 'listener'. Ask the talker to talk for 2 – 3 minutes (e.g. about a hobby, a recent holiday or what they did at the weekend). The other person just listens – when the time is up they will have to feed back to the group the key points that the talker mentioned.

2. Once the time is up, ask the listeners feed back the main points of what was said. This can be to the whole group or, if time is an issue, they can just tell their partner. It doesn't matter if listeners can only remember one or two things.

3. Next, ask the listeners what they found difficult about the task. What made it difficult for them to listen? Perhaps there was too much background noise? Maybe their thoughts were elsewhere? Maybe they did not understand what the other person was saying? Maybe they remember best when they make notes? During this reflection, see if any individuals can suggest helpful strategies to cope with these difficulties (e.g. moving to a quieter location,

seeking clarification when something is said that they do not understand).

4. Swap roles and complete steps 1–3 again so that all participants have a chance to reflect on their listening skills.

5. You might follow up this activity by asking participants at a later date whether they have had an opportunity to put any strategies into place in other contexts.

COMMUNICATION SKILLS

Aim: To identify effective communication skills and identify areas to develop further.

How to do it:

1. Divide the group into pairs. Give one person from each pair a 'Card A' from Appendix H and the other person a 'Card B'. The two are not to show or tell each other what is on the card.

2. Tell group members to follow the instruction that is on their card. Participants might prefer to do this in their pairs, but an alternative is for each pair to do their role-play in front of the rest of the group. Allow 2–3 minutes for participants to do their role-play. You might like to give each group time to do several of the role-plays and to take it in turns being 'A' and 'B'.

3. Tell the group that they were acting out poor listening and communication skills in their role-plays. Can they identify what these were? What could be better to do instead, and why?

4. As an extension to this activity, individuals might like to complete the 'Communication Self-Audit', which is

provided in Appendix I and also forms the basis of one of the individual activities. Help individuals to identify possible strategies that they could try out (e.g. looking at a person's forehead if eye contact is uncomfortable, or facing their body towards that person).

ASSERTIVENESS SKILLS

Aim: To identify the difference between aggressive, passive and assertive communication skills, to encourage more positive interactions with others.

How to do it:

1. Explain that we can respond to a situation in one of three ways: aggressively, passively or assertively. Explain what each type of response looks like.

    • An aggressive response can involve anger, violence and physical or verbal attacks. It might include sarcasm or an attempt to hurt the other person in some way. An aggressive response does not respect other people and may include shouting, swearing, threatening, or acting as if you are better than others.

    • A passive response often involves saying or doing nothing. It lacks confidence and avoids the problem. A passive response involves keeping your feelings to yourself and allowing others to treat you with disrespect. You may speak quietly, say nothing, make yourself look small, go along with things you are uncomfortable with, or act as if you are not as important as other people.

    • An assertive response, however, is in the middle of these two extremes. It involves expressing your thoughts and feelings honestly and openly. It respects both yourself and the other person and allows you to exercise your personal rights without denying the rights of others.

2. Ask the group to work in threes. Give each group a set of the cards in Appendix G. Ask one member of the group first to act out an aggressive response to the situation. Once they have finished, the next person acts out a passive response, and then the third acts out an assertive response. Individuals who do not enjoy role-play may prefer simply to talk about what that sort of response would look and sound like. Some tips for an assertive response include:

- Keep calm and use a low, clear and steady voice.

- Stand up tall and still.

- Look at the other person to show you are listening to their point of view.

- Use 'I' statements to describe how you feel ('I feel… when you…because…'; 'I would like…').

- Respect your own feelings and those of other people

- Do not feel that you have to keep justifying your reasons; just remain polite and firm

3. Take feedback from the groups and support those who struggled to imagine some of the different responses.

4. Extend this activity by asking whether there are any real-life situations in which individuals feel they have responded too aggressively or passively. This is an opportunity to discuss more assertive responses in a supportive atmosphere.

AUTISM-FRIENDLY ENVIRONMENTS

Aim: To help to create more autism-friendly environment in the local community

How to do it: The concept of 'autism-friendly environments' has gained prominence in recent years and there may already be autism-friendly spaces in your local area.

1. With the group, generate a list of public spaces in your local area that group members use, or would like to use. You might include:

    • Community centres

    • Sports centres

    • Leisure centres

    • Libraries

    • Other sporting and fitness facilities

    • Medical centres

    • Dentist's surgery

    • Shopping centres

    • Pubs, bars, cafés and restaurants

    • Shops

    • Colleges or adult learning centres

    • Day centres

2. Depending on the group and number of places identified, you might wish to complete the activity as a whole group, or divide the group into twos or threes, giving one place to each group. Ask each group to consider how far they believe the place is autism-friendly. They should list the

good points, and the more negative ones. For each negative, try to generate possible solutions to the problem (e.g. providing a quiet space).

3. Feed back to the whole group, asking others to add to the lists. No two individuals on the autism spectrum are the same, so there is likely to be a range of (perhaps conflicting) opinions. Try to come up with a list that reflects the variety of needs for individuals on the autism spectrum.

4. Once these steps have been completed, decide how you are going to use this information to improve local services for individuals on the autism spectrum. The group might decide to write a letter or email about their thoughts to the service or organisation in question. Others might want to arrange a face-to-face meeting, or present their findings at a local town council meeting if possible. You might wish to invite representatives of various services into your group meetings for them to find out more about the needs of those on the autism spectrum. There are further details on autism-friendly environments on the National Autistic Society website (see the 'Further Reading and Resources' section in this book).

WHAT'S IMPORTANT TO ME?

Aim: To identify what things are important to individuals within the group and how they can be used to increase happiness, meaning and purpose.

How to do it:

1. Ask each member of the group to answer the question 'What is important to you?' Some might like to draw a spider diagram or make a collage, others might like to

write their answers, while some might prefer to discuss their thoughts. Examples of prompts are animals, your environment, your home, work, your lifestyle, hobbies and interests, causes close to your heart, issues you feel are important.

2. You might also like to give the list of values in the 'Values Clarifier' activity. Facilitate feedback after an appropriate amount of time, for those who would like to share their thoughts. Highlight that we all have different things that are important to us, and all are equally valid.

3. An extension of this activity could be to support group members to align their life more with their values and what is important to them. If, for example, an individual states that nature, the environment and being outdoors is very important to them, yet lives in a small inner-city flat and spends all their time indoors, help them to seek out opportunities to do more of the things that are important to them.

REFERENCES

Attwood, T. (2007) *The Complete Guide to Asperger Syndrome.* London: Jessica Kingsley Publishers.

Baylis, N. (2009) *The Rough Guide to Happiness.* London: Rough Guides Ltd.

Bergland (2014) 'Can reading a fictional story make you more empathetic?' *Psychology Today.* Available at www.psychologytoday.com/blog/the-athletes-way/201412/can-reading-fictional-story-make-you-more-empathetic, accessed on 15 July 2018.

Billstedt, E., Gillberg, C. and Gillberg, C. (2011) 'Aspects of quality of life in adults diagnosed with autism in childhood: A population-based study.' Sage Publications and the National Autistic Society. Available at www.gnc.gu.se/digitalAssets/1349/1349896_billstedt-aspects-of-quality-of-life.pdf, accessed on 15 July 2018.

Blanden, J. (2006) '"Bucking the Trend": What enables those who are disadvantaged in childhood to succeed later in life?' Working Paper 31. London: Department for Work and Pensions.

Blyth, L. (2013) *The Secrets of Happiness: How to Love Life, Laugh More and Live Longer.* London: CICO books.

Bogdashina, O. (2013) *Autism and Spirituality.* London: Jessica Kingsley Publishers.

Boniwell, I. (2008) *Positive Psychology in a Nutshell* (second edition). London: PWBC.

Boniwell, I. (2015) 'Setting them up for a happy future.' *Psychologies,* August 2015.

Boniwell, I. and Ryan, L. (2012) *Personal Well-being Lessons for Secondary Schools: Positive Psychology in Action.* Maidenhead: Open University Press.

Burton, N. (2013) 'Aristotle on happiness', *Psychology Today,* 28 January 2013. Available at www.psychologytoday.com/us/blog/hide-and-seek/201301/aristotle-happiness, accessed on 15 July 2018.

Carr, N. (2010) *The Shallows: What the Internet Is Doing to Our Brain.* New York, NY: Norton.

Clifton, D. and Anderson, E. (2001) *StrengthsQuest.* Washington, DC: The Gallup Organization.

Csikszentmihalyi, M, (1992) *Flow: The Psychology of Happiness.* London: Rider.

Danner, D., Snowdon, D. and Friedsen, W. (2001) Positive emotions early in life and the longevity: Findings from the nun study.' *Journal of Personality and Social Psychology 80,* 804–813.

Deci, E.L. and Ryan, R.M. (1985) *Intrinsic Motivation and Self-Determination in Human Behavior.* New York, NY: Plenum.

Dweck, C. (2006) *Mindset: The New Psychology of Success*. New York, NY: Balantine Books.

Easterlin, R. (2008). 'Income and happiness: Towards a unified theory.' *The Economic Journal. 11*(473), 465–484.

Emmons, R. (2007) *Thanks! How the New Science of Gratitude Can Make You Happier*. New York, NY: Houghton-Mifflin.

Esfahani Smith, E. (2017) *The Power of Meaning: Crafting a Life That Matters*. New York, NY: Crown Publishing Group.

Fredrickson, B. (2009) *Positivity*. New York, NY: Crown Publishers.

Fredrickson, B.L. and Joiner, T. (2002) 'Positive emotions trigger upward spirals toward emotional well-being.' *Psychological Science 13*, 172–175.

Fredrickson, B.L., Mancuso, R.A, Branigan, C. and Tugade, M.M. (2000) 'The undoing effect of positive emotions.' *Motivation and Emotion 24*, 237–258.

Gardner, H. and Davis, K. (2013) *The App Generation*. New Haven, CT: Yale University Press.

Gillberg, I.C., Råstam, M. and Gillberg, C. (1995). 'Anorexia nervosa 6 years after onset.' *Comprehensive Psychiatry 36*(1), 61–69.

Gould, J. and Ashton-Smith, J. (2011) 'Missed diagnosis or misdiagnosis? Girls and women on the autism spectrum.' *Good Autism Practice Journal 12*, 34–41.

Govindji, R. and Linley, P.A. (2007) 'Strengths use, self-concordance and well-being: Implications for strengths coaching and coaching psychologists.' *International Coaching Psychology Review 2*(2), 143–153.

Hanson, R, (2013) *Hardwiring Happiness: The Practical Science of Reshaping Your Brain – and Your Life*. London: Ebury Publishing.

Hudson, C., Hall, L. and Harkness, K. (2018) 'Prevalence of depressive disorders in individuals with autism spectrum disorder: A meta-analysis.' *Journal of Abnormal Child Psychology*. Available at https://doi.org/10.1007/s10802-018-0402-1, accessed on 15 July 2018.

Hurley, E. (2014) *Ultraviolet Voices: Stories of Women on the Autism Spectrum*. Birmingham: Autism West Midlands.

Ifcher, J. and Zarghamee, H. (2011) 'Positive affect and overconfidence: A laboratory investigation.' *SCU Leavey School of Business Research Paper No 11-02*. Available at http://ssrn.com/abstract=1740013, accessed on 15 July 2018.

Jamison, T.R. and Schuttler, J.O. (2015) 'Examining social competence, self-perception, quality of life and internalising and externalising symptoms in adolescent females with and without autism spectrum disorders: A quantitative design including between-groups and correlational analyses.' *Molecular Autism 17*, 6–53.

Judge, T.A. and Hurst, C. (2007) 'Capitalising on one's advantage: role of core self-evaluations.' *Journal of Applied Psychology 92*, 1212–1227.

Kaufman, B. (1991) *Happiness Is a Choice*. New York, NY: Ballantine.

Khanna, R., Jariwala-Parikh, K., West-Strum, D. and Mahabaleshwarkar, R. (2014) 'Health related quality of life and its determinants among adults with autism.' *Research in Autism Spectrum Disorders 8*, 157–167.

Kim, J.A., Szatmari, P., Bryson, S., Streiner D.L. and Wilson, F. (2000) 'The prevalence of anxiety and mood problems among children with autism and Asperger Syndrome.' *Autism: The International Journal of Research and Practice 4*(2), 117–132.

King, V. (2015) 'Why goals make us happy.' *Psychologies*, August 2015.

King, V. (2017) 'Meaning mindset.' *Psychologies*, June 2017.

Kutscher, M. (2016) *Digital Kids: How to Balance Screen Time and Why It Matters.* London: Jessica Kingsley Publishers.

Kuzmanovic, B., Rigoux, L. and Vogeley, K. (2016) 'Brief report: reduced optimism bias in self-referential belief updating in high functioning autism.' *Journal of Autism and Developmental Disorders.* Published online 18 October 2016, available at https://link.springer.com/article/10.1007%2Fs10803-016-2940-0, accessed on 15 July 2018.

LeBon, T. (2014) *Achieve Your Potential with Positive Psychology.* London: Hodder & Stoughton.

Linley, P.A. (2008) *From Average to A+.* Warwick: CAPP Press.

Linley, P.A., Nielsen, K.M., Wood, K.M., Gillett, R. and Biswas-Diener, R. (2010) 'Using signature strengths in pursuit of goals: Effects on goal progress, need satisfaction and well-being, and implications for coaching psychologists.' *International Coaching Psychology Review 5*(1), 8–17.

Lyubomirsky, S. (2007) *The How of Happiness.* London: Sphere.

Lyubomirsky, S., King, L. and Diener, E. (2005) 'The benefits of frequent positive affect: Does happiness lead to success?' *Psychological Bulletin 131*, 803–855.

Lyubomirsky, S., Sheldon, K.M. and Schkade, D. (2005) 'Pursuing happiness: The architecture of sustainable change.' *Review of General Psychology 9*(2), 111–131.

Mayor, S. (2017) 'One to two hours of exercise each week nearly halves long term risk of depression.' *BMJ* 2017 359:j4534. Available at www.bmj.com/content/359/bmj.j4534, accessed on 15 July 2018.

McDonell, A. and Milton, D. (2014) 'Going with the flow: Reconsidering repetitive behaviour through the concept of flow states.' *Good Autism Practice Journal: Happiness, Autism and Wellbeing*, September 2014, 38–47.

McKay, S. (2014) 'Why crafting is great for your brain: A neuroscientist explains.' Available at www.mindbodygreen.com/0-14252/why-crafting-is-great-for-your-brain-a-neuroscientist-explains.html, accessed on 15 July 2018.

McLeod, A., Coates, E. and Hetherton, J. (2008) 'Increasing well-being through teaching goal-setting and planning skills: Results of a brief intervention.' *Journal of Happiness Studies 9*(2), 185–196.

Mechelli, A. (2018) 'Urban mind: Using smartphone technologies to investigate the impact of nature on mental wellbeing in real time.' *BioScience 68*(2), 134–145.

Minhas, G. (2010) 'Developing realised and unrealised strengths: Implications for engagement, self-esteem, life satisfaction and well-being.' *Assessment and Development Matters 2*, 12–16.

National Autistic Society (NAS) (2016a) 'Autism: What is autism?' Available at www.autism.org.uk/about/what-is/asd.aspx, accessed on 15 July 2018.

National Autistic Society (NAS) (2016b) 'Eating.' Available at www.autism.org.uk/about/health/eating.aspx, accessed on 5 July 2018.

Ni, P. (2014) 'How to stop comparing yourself to others and feel happier.' *Psychology Today*. Available at www.psychologytoday.com/us/blog/communication-success/201409/how-stop-comparing-yourself-others-and-feel-happier, accessed on 15 July 2018.

Office for National Statistics (ONS) (2016) 'Measuring national wellbeing: At what age is personal wellbeing the highest?' Available at www.ons.gov.uk/peoplepopulationandcommunity/wellbeing/articles/measuringnationalwellbeing/atwhatageispersonalwellbeingthehighest, accessed on 15 July 2018.

Park, N. and Peterson, C. (2006) Moral competence and character strengths among adolescents: The development and validation of the Values in Action Inventory of Strengths for Youth. *Journal of Adolescence 29*, 891–909.

Peterson, C. and Park N. (2003) 'Positive psychology as the even-handed positive psychologist views it.' *Psychological Enquiry 14*, 115–120.

Rae, T. (2016) *The Wellbeing Toolkit*. London: Nurture Group Network

Rae, T. and MacConville, R. (2015) *Using Positive Psychology to Enhance Student Achievement: A Schools-Based Programme for Character Education*. Abingdon: Routledge.

Reading Agency (2016) *The Untold Power of the Book*. Available at https://readingagency.org.uk/news/GALAXY%20Quick%20Reads%20Report%202016%20FINAL.pdf, accessed on 15 July 2018.

Renty J. and Roeyers H. (2006) 'Satisfaction with formal support and education for children with autism spectrum disorder: The voices of the parents.' *Child Care and Health Development 32*(3),371–385.

Roberts, M (2015) 'Write your thoughts in a diary.' *Psychologies* August 2015.

Rowe, A. (2015) *Asperger Syndrome: Social Energy: By the Girl with the Curly Hair.* CreateSpace.

Seligman, M. (2002) *Authentic Happiness*. New York, NY: The Free Press.

Seligman, M., (2011) *Flourish: A New Understanding of Happiness and Well-Being and How to Achieve Them*. London: Nicholas Brearley Publishing.

Seligman, M. and Csikszentmihalyi, M. (2000) 'Positive psychology: An introduction.' *American Psychologist 55*, 5–14.

Seligman, M., Steen, T., Park, N. and Peterson, P. (2005) Positive psychology progress: Empirical validation of interventions.' *American Psychologist 60*(5), 410–421.

Simone, R. (2010) *Aspergirls: Empowering Females with Asperger Syndrome*. London: Jessica Kingsley Publishers.

Snyder, C.R. (2000) *Handbook of Hope*. Orlando, FL: Academic Press.

Solomon, M., Miller, M., Taylor, S.L., Hinshaw, S. and Carter, C.S. (2012) 'Autism symptoms and internalising psychopathology in girls and boys with autism spectrum disorders.' *Journal of Autism and Developmental Disorders 42*, 48–59.

Van Heijst, B. and Geurts, H. (2014) 'Quality of life in autism across the lifespan: A meta-analysis.' *Autism 19*(2), 158–167

Van Wijngaarden-Cremers, P.J., Van Eeten, E., Groen, W.B., Van Deurzen, P.A., Oosterling, I.J. and Van Der Gaag, R.J. (2014) 'Gender and age differences in the core triad of impairments in autism spectrum disorders: A systematic review and meta-analysis.' *Journal of Autism and Developmental Disorders 44*, 627–635.

Vermeulen, P. (2014) 'The Practice of Promoting Happiness in Autism.' In Jones, G. and Hurley, E. *Good Autism Practice*. Birmingham: BILD. Available at www.researchgate. net/publication/269072830_The_practice_of_promoting_happiness_in_autism, accessed on 15 July 2018.

Vermeulen, P. (2016) 'Promoting happiness in autistic people.' Network Autism. Available at https://network.autism.org.uk/knowledge/insight-opinion/ promoting-happiness-autistic-people, accessed on 15 July 2018.

Weldon, J. (2014) *Can I tell you about Autism? A guide for friends, family and professionals.* London: Jessica Kingsley Publishing.

Wells, D. (2011) 'The value of pets in human health.' *The Psychologist 24*(3), 172–176.

Wilson, T.D. (2011) *Redirect: The Surprising New Science of Psychological Change.* London: Allen Lane.

Yalom, I. (1989) *Love's Executioner.* London: Penguin.

FURTHER READING AND RESOURCES

POSITIVE PSYCHOLOGY

Boniwell, I. (2008) *Positive Psychology in a Nutshell.* London: PWBC.

Carr, A. (2004) *Positive Psychology.* Hove: Brunner-Routledge.

Csikszentmihalyi, M. (1992) *Flow: The Psychology of Happiness.* London: Rider.

Gray, C. (2015) *The New Social Story Book.* Arlington, TX: Future Horizons Firm.

Peterson, C. and Seligman, M. (2004) *Character Strengths and Virtues: A Handbook and Classification.* New York, NY: Oxford University Press.

Snyder, C.R. and Lopez, S.J. (2002) *Handbook of Positive Psychology.* New York, NY: Oxford University Press.

POSITIVE PSYCHOLOGY ORGANISATIONS

European Network of Positive Psychology (ENPP)

enpp.eu

International Positive Psychology Association (IPPA)

www.ippanetwork.org

Personal Wellbeing Centre

www.personalwellbeingcentre.org

Positive Psychology Center, University of Pennsylvania

www.ppc.sas.upenn.edu

Positive Psychology UK

http://positivepsychology.org.uk/home.html

University of Cambridge Well-being Institute

www.cambridgewellbeing.org

Via Character Strengths Survey

Viacharacter.org

Gallup Strengths Center

Gallupstrengthscenter.com

AUTISM

Attwood, T. (2007) *The Complete Guide to Asperger Syndrome*. London: Jessica Kingsley Publishers.

Baron-Cohen, S. (2008) *The Facts: Autism and Asperger Syndrome*. Oxford: Oxford University Press.

Gray, C. Social Stories™ and comic strip conversations. Visit http://carolgraysocialstories.com.

Silberman, S. (2015) *Neurotribes: The Legacy of Autism and How to Think Smarter about People Who Think Differently*. Australia: Allen & Unwin.

Vermeulen P. (2012) *Autism as Context Blindness*. Kansas: AAPC Publishing.

Willey, L.H. (2015) *Pretending to be Normal: Living with Asperger Syndrome* (second edition). London: Jessica Kingsley Publishers.

AUTISM SUPPORT ORGANISATIONS

Ambitious About Autism

www.ambitiousaboutautism.org.uk

American Asperger Association

http://americanaspergers.forumotion.net

Asperger Syndrome Foundation

www.aspergerfoundation.org.uk

Autism New Zealand

www.autismnz.org.nz

Autism Society Canada

www.autismcanada.org

Autism Spectrum Australia

www.autismspectrum.org.au

Autism West Midlands

www.autismwestmidlands.org.uk

National Autistic Society
www.autism.org.uk

US Autism and Asperger Association
www.usautism.org

FURTHER RESOURCES AND SUPPORT

NHS Choices
Nhs.uk

JobCentre
Gov.uk/jobsearch

Samaritans
Samaritans.org

Citizens Advice Bureau
Citizensadvice.org.uk

Money Advice Service
Moneyadviceservice.org.uk

Government services and organisations
Gov.uk

Access to Work
Gov.uk/access-to-work

APPENDICES

The Appendices are available to download and print from www.jkp.com/voucher using the code DYYVERE

Appendix A

STRENGTHS AND DEFINITIONS

Can you match the words with their definitions?

Strength	Definition
Enthusiastic	Being original and finding new ways of doing things
Self-control	Being hopeful and looking for positive things
Grateful	Continuing to try, even though things may be difficult or you face setbacks
Persevering	Being thankful for good things in your life and positive things that happen
Creative	Doing things with energy and enthusiasm
Optimistic	Controlling your thinking and behaviour when it is necessary
Forgiving	Respecting and considering other people's opinions and points of view; not jumping to conclusions or being prejudiced
Honest	Doing nice things for other people, caring and looking out for others
Reliable	Being trusted to do something and knowing the difference between right and wrong
Kind	Forgiving people when they have made a mistake and giving them a second chance
Leadership	You can be trusted to do what you say you will do
Responsible	Directing and organising tasks or events and encouraging others to join in
Open-minded	Telling the truth
Spirituality	Giving everybody a fair chance, regardless of your personal opinions

Strength	Definition
Love of learning	Being interested in new things and asking questions
Independent	Getting on well with others in social situations
Curious	Enjoy gaining new knowledge and finding out new things
Generous	Working well within a group of people
Team Work	Being able to do things by yourself
Sociable	Sharing your time, belongings or effort with others
Humour	Being able to see the funny side of things
Fair	Believing in something 'bigger' than yourself – perhaps a religion
Modesty	Believing in equal rights and justice for all, regardless of background or other differences
Patience	Being aware of, understanding and managing your emotions well
Authentic	Being able to evaluate a problem from different perspectives
Organisation	Not 'showing off' or boasting
Critical thinking	Being able to wait calmly and not expecting things immediately
Emotional intelligence	Being organised – having the right things and knowing what is coming up
Adaptable	Being yourself, not just copying others but doing what is important to you
Equality	Being flexible and able to adapt to different circumstances

Answers:

Word	Definition
Creative	Being original and finding new ways of doing things
Optimistic	Being hopeful and looking for positive things
Persevering	Continuing to try, even though things may be difficult or you face setbacks
Grateful	Being thankful for good things in your life and positive things that happen
Enthusiastic	Doing things with energy and enthusiasm
Self-control	Controlling your thinking and behaviour when it is necessary
Open-minded	Respecting and considering other people's opinions and points of view; not jumping to conclusions or being prejudiced
Kind	Doing nice things for other people, caring and looking out for others
Responsible	Being trusted to do something and knowing the difference between right and wrong
Forgiving	Forgiving people when they have made a mistake and giving them a second chance
Reliable	You can be trusted to do what you say you will do
Leadership	Directing and organising tasks or events and encouraging others to join in
Honest	Telling the truth
Fair	Giving everybody a fair chance, regardless of your personal opinions
Curious	Being interested in new things and asking questions
Sociable	Getting on well with others in social situations
Love of learning	Enjoy gaining new knowledge and finding out new things
Team work	Working well within a group of people
Independent	Being able to do things by yourself
Generous	Sharing your time, belongings or effort with others
Humour	Being able to see the funny side of things

Word	Definition
Spirituality	Believing in something 'bigger' than yourself – perhaps a religion
Equality	Believing in equal rights and justice for all, regardless of background or other differences
Emotional intelligence	Being aware of, understanding and managing your emotions well
Critical thinking	Being able to evaluate a problem from different perspectives
Modesty	Not 'showing off' or boasting
Patience	Being able to wait calmly and not expecting things immediately
Organisation	Being organised – having the right things and knowing what is coming up
Authentic	Being yourself, not just copying others but doing what is important to you
Adaptable	Being flexible and able to adapt to different circumstances

Appendix B

FIXED OR GROWTH MINDSET?

Fixed mindset	Growth mindset
I'm no good at maths.	I can get better at this.
I can't do DIY.	I'm still learning how to do this.
I'm brilliant at driving.	I can't do this yet but I will get better at it.
I give up.	I'm improving at this.
I won't be able to do this.	I've learned from my mistakes.
I don't have a brain for languages.	This could be a challenge but I'll use it as an opportunity.
I'll never be able to ride a bicycle.	I'm going to try hard at this.
I'll never get better at this. There's no point trying.	I can try another way.
I got really bad feedback. This obviously isn't for me.	It's OK to make mistakes; that's how we learn.
I'll avoid that; I'll only fail anyway.	I can learn from this experience.
I'm good at this; I don't need to try hard.	I like a challenge.
I couldn't do this last time I tried; I won't be able to this time	I can keep trying.

Appendix C

MY SENSORY PROFILE

Sense	My differences	My coping strategies
Sight/visual		
Sound		
Smell		
Taste		
Texture		
Balance		
Motor skills		
Body awareness		

Appendix D

SOCIAL MEDIA

Do you think the following statements are positive or negative?

Through social media you can keep in touch with family and friends.	Using social media means you can meet new people from around the world.	Social media is an easy way of sharing photos and videos of your private life.
Through social media you can keep up to date with news and what is going on in the world.	Social media is an easy way of communicating with people.	Through social media you can stay informed about what your friends and family are doing.
Social media is a place you can ask for advice and find information.	Social media is a place you can share your thoughts and feelings.	Social media allows you to say things that you cannot in 'real' life.
Social media is a way of finding out what is going on in your local community and friendship circles.	On social media you can connect with like-minded people.	Users can post what they like on social media – there is freedom to express yourself.

Social media scenarios

Somebody posts an unflattering photo of you showing you in a drunken state on a night out. You are tagged in it. What do you do?

You see your friendship group has posted photos of a social event they went to, which you knew nothing about and would have liked to have been invited to. What do you do?

One of your friends makes a derogatory comment online about all autistic people. What do you do?

You read an item in your newsfeed about autism and are worried about what it is implying. What do you do?

Somebody makes a political comment on social media. You have quite strong political views and disagree with the person. What do you do?

You have started to chat to somebody you do not know online. They suggest meeting up. What do you do?

Somebody you do not know is asking you to add them as a friend on your social media sites. What do you do?

You have posted an opinion and two other people reply with comments saying you are wrong. What do you do?

You are having an online conversation with a friend and one of them posts something that you think is a criticism of you. What do you do?

You post a comment and photo but then begin to worry that you have shared too much. What do you do?

You are scrolling through your newsfeeds and see your friends posting about their busy social life. They all seem to be busy, enjoying themselves and having more fun than you. You begin to feel unhappy. What do you do?

You are trying to talk to somebody online but they are not replying to any of your messages. What do you do?

A colleague posts something negative about you. What do you do?

A stranger begins an argument with you on Twitter. What do you do?

★

Appendix E

OPTIMISM AND PESSIMISM

Discuss optimistic and pessimistic responses to each of the following situations:

You have made some new friends at a sports club you go to and wonder if they would like to go for coffee and cake one day after training.	You see a job advertised, which you feel you would be well suited to, and wonder whether to apply.	A friend has invited you to a party to celebrate their birthday.
Your boss said that he would like to speak to you about something and has arranged a meeting with you later in the week.	You are told that you will have to move out of your flat as the building is being sold.	A community centre that you use frequently is going to close down next month.
You have to get a qualification at work so that you can continue in the role.	You have been successful getting a new job but it is in a new town and you think you will have to move there.	You meet somebody you like and wonder whether to invite them on a date.
You have always been interested in dance and see that there is an adults' dance class starting up nearby.		

★

Appendix F

UNHOPEFUL STATEMENTS

Can you rephrase these statements so that they are more hopeful?

Statement	More hopeful statement
I'll never be able to drive a car.	
I'll never find a partner.	
I don't have a chance of getting a new job because of my autism.	
I never understand what my colleagues are saying.	
I find lunchtimes at work boring.	
I'm too nervous to go along to a craft club.	
I made a mess of working on the tills last time I tried it.	
I disagreed with a colleague today; he will never be friendly to me again.	
The course I am studying is too hard.	
My support worker won't be able to help me.	
I find support groups boring; I won't go along to the new one that is starting up.	
I'll never be able to live independently.	

★

AGGRESSIVE, PASSIVE AND ASSERTIVE RESPONSES

You have to take some faulty goods back to a shop for a refund.	You are given a meal in a restaurant but it is not what you ordered.	A colleague blames you for something you did not do.
You get a phone call on your mobile from somebody trying to sell you something you do not want.	Somebody knocks at your front door, asking you to make a donation to charity.	You have been to a job interview and the employer calls you to say you have not been successful.
You are waiting for a dental appointment and it is now 45 minutes after your appointment time. You think you may have been forgotten.	You have parked in the sports' centre car park, but when you come to drive home you realise somebody has blocked you in and you cannot back your car out.	Two of your colleagues are talking about autism in very negative terms.
Your work coach at the job centre suggests you apply for a supermarket job, but you know you would find the environment overwhelming.		

Appendix H

COMMUNICATION SKILLS ROLE-PLAYS

Person A	Person B
A: Start up a conversation with your partner about what you have both done at the weekend.	**B:** Give only 'yes' or 'no' answers to your partner. Do not ask any questions of your own.
A: Talk to your partner about a hobby or interest that you have.	**B:** While your partner is talking, walk around the room and look at other things.
A: Start a conversation by talking to your partner about your favourite TV show, favourite book or favourite music.	**B:** While your partner is talking, try to look very bored. Look at your watch or get your phone out. Fiddle with other objects. Look around the room. Yawn loudly.
A: Start up a conversation with your partner about the town that you live in, what there is to do and whether or not you like it.	**B:** While your partner is talking to you, try to keep changing the subject – talk about one of your hobbies and interests.

Person A	Person B
A: Tell your partner about a hobby or interest that you have.	**B:** When your partner starts talking, keep interrupting them with unrelated comments.
A: Start up a conversation with your partner about anything that you are interested in or want to talk about.	**B:** Ask your partner lots of questions as they are talking and do not give them time to answer the questions properly.
A: Try to find out from your partner what they did at the weekend or during a recent holiday.	**B:** Join in the conversation but give only single-word answers such as 'yes' or 'no'. Do not ask any questions.

Appendix I

COMMUNICATION SKILLS SELF-AUDIT

	I am not very confident doing this	I could do with more practice at this	I can usually do this well	I do this very well
I use appropriate eye contact with other people.				
My body language shows that I am listening to others.				
I use facial expression to show I am listening and to add meaning to what I am saying.				
My hand gestures are appropriate.				
I do not stand too far away or too close to others.				
I speak at an appropriate volume – not too loudly and not too quietly.				
I speak at an appropriate pace – not too quickly and not too slowly.				

	I am not very confident doing this	I could do with more practice at this	I can usually do this well	I do this very well
I speak clearly.				
I vary my tone of voice to make my speech more interesting.				
I use words that others understand.				
I know how to start a conversation.				
I know how to end a conversation.				
I can keep a conversation going.				
I know when it is my turn to speak.				
I can interrupt politely.				
I know how to change the topic of conversation appropriately.				
I listen to what others say and respond appropriately.				
I ask others appropriate questions.				
I answer questions appropriately.				
I seek clarification when I do not understand.				

I can express my thoughts clearly.				
I understand what others are saying.				
I help others to contribute to the conversation.				
I move the conversation forward, rather than repeating the same thing.				
I take other people's feelings and opinions into consideration.				
I avoid offending others.				
I use an appropriate level of formality and politeness.				

INDEX OF ACTIVITIES

INDEX